Life
is a
Conversation

Life is a Conversation

The Writings and Art of
Janet Franklin Foster

Compiled and Introduced by
Richard Foster

St. Lynn's Press
Pittsburgh

Life is a Conversation

Copyright © 2017
by Richard J. W. Foster

All rights reserved. No part of this book may be reproduced, stored, or transmitted in any form without permission in writing from the publisher, except by a reviewer who may quote brief passages for review purposes.

ISBN-13: 978-1-943366-34-7

Library of Congress Control Number: 2017948339
CIP information available upon request

First Edition, 2017

St. Lynn's Press
POB 18680 . Pittsburgh, PA 15236
412.381.9933 . www.stlynnspress.com

Book design – Holly Rosborough
Editor – Catherine Dees

Photo credits:
All photos © Richard Foster, with the exception of the following:
© Janet Franklin Foster: pages 87, 179, 181, 182, 201;
© Laura Franklin: pages 33, 121 and back cover photo;
© Todd Volkmer: Janet's art images on pages 11, 21, 39, 47, 55, 73, 75, 77, 99, 144, 157, 161, 177, 188, 192, 211, 215;
© Rob Hartshorn: Janet's art images on pages 37, 88, 110, 118, 141, 171, 173, 191, 216;
© Dorcas Foster: page 218

Printed in Canada
On certified FSC paper using soy-based inks

10 9 8 7 6 5 4 3 2 1

To Janet

CONTENTS

9   Introduction

12   Toronto Conversations

34   Everyday Conversations

62   Nature Conversations

92   Cottage Conversations

112   Molokai Conversations

134   Family Conversations

174   Cancer Conversations

220   Acknowledgments

222   About the Author

Introduction

The book you hold in your hands is the completion of a commitment I made to myself when my wife lost her seven-year battle with breast cancer on March 9, 2017. On that day, and every day since, I have needed a reason to keep living on without Janet's physical presence; and although the process of pulling together writings from Janet's portfolio of completed poems and from her many journals has been the most profoundly painful emotional experience of my life, it has also been an amazing gift to me of deeper clarity and insight into the richness of our life together – and a greater sense of gratitude for the rare depth of love and connection we shared. And it's my wish that you will be as blessed in your life, as I have been blessed by my eighteen-year life with Janet.

At times while working on Janet's book I felt that I couldn't continue any further in the task I'd set out for myself…only to receive dramatic signs of Janet's loving and nurturing spirit presence, which encouraged me to keep on with the work. In persevering, I have been gifted with periods of peace and gratitude for Janet's spirit, and God's grace. I have no doubt that these experiences – which I call *God Moments* of His direct presence in my life – brought us together eighteen years ago to demonstrate His love and compassion for us, and to give each of us a time of great joy and shared growth.

My hope is that you will experience some of Janet's life energy through her writings...conversations that flow throughout the pages of her book, speaking to you about her pure sense of joy, her humor, intelligence, creativity and faith. It is also my hope that you will laugh and weep and celebrate her life with me, even though the writings and artwork in this book give only a small glimpse into the complexity of Janet's beautiful spirit. I pray that Janet's light will shine through these pages into your mind and into your heart.

This book is my gift to family and friends. May your love for my wife continue to grow through her writings as you move forward with the remainder of your lives. And to those who only know the name Janet Franklin Foster, and those who acquired this book by choice, or by fate: May you experience what Janet expressed in one of her writings...the softness and magic of a hummingbird's breath. And may the experience of only one such moment on a single page open the energy of your heart, and your special gifts, to all you touch.

Richard Foster
September 23, 2017

Note: At the start of each chapter you will find a listing of each of Janet's writings within that chapter, along with my own annotations to provide context.

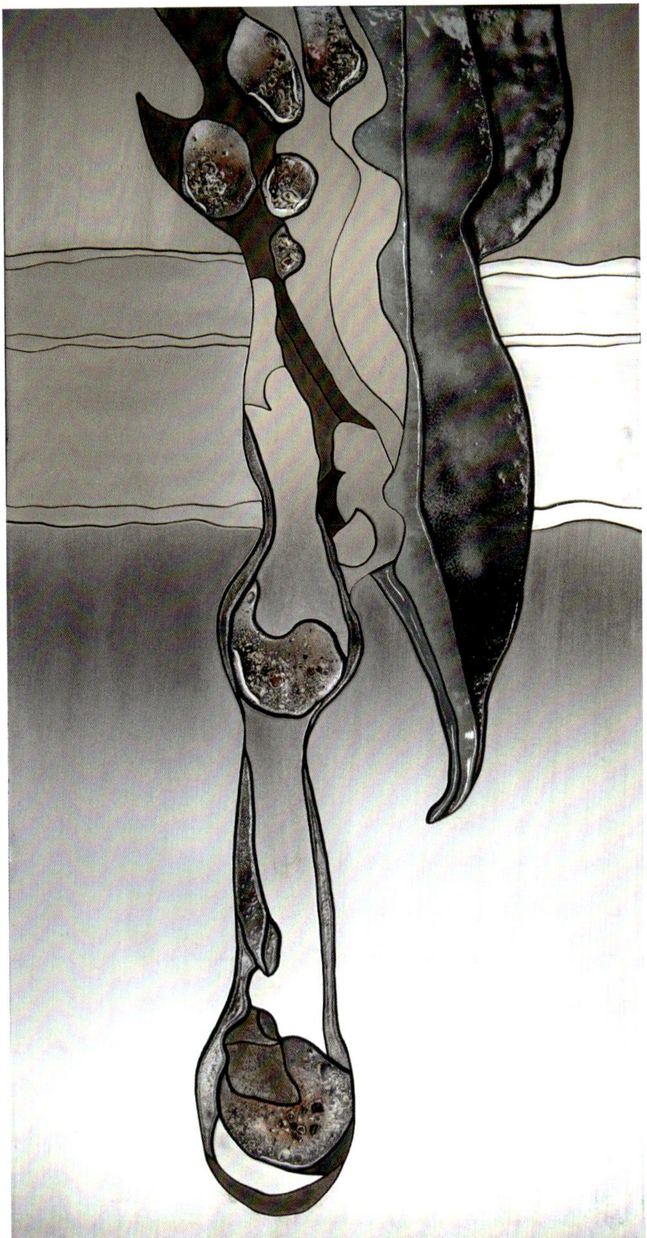

TORONTO CONVERSATIONS

Janet and I first met at a cousin's wedding reception in Toronto the summer of 1996. While enjoying the reception and reconnecting with my Toronto cousins my eyes were drawn to a dark-haired woman crossing the dance floor…and I followed. When I caught up with her, she was standing alone at a table of wedding favors, trying to choose between two spruce tree seedlings: Should she select the "perfect one," she asked me, or the spindly one. I suggested she take both. Advice she considered, then chose to rescue the one in need of TLC. After our brief conversation, I returned to join my cousins. I asked for the name of this beautiful woman, and was told to forget about it because her husband had died suddenly a year earlier and she was still deep in grief. And so I dismissed any further thoughts about her. Two years later, on a blind date arranged by one of my sons and a cousin, I arrived at the front door of a Toronto home to see Janet standing there. "You're the one!" I exclaimed. She said, "What do you mean?" And I said, "Well, you're the one I crossed the wedding dance floor to meet two years ago." She didn't recall our first meeting. But that's how our love story began.

14 *A Single Blossom* – Janet's love poem to me.

15 *A Whirlwind Tour* – About an early moment in our relationship.

16 *Dear Richard* – Janet's birthday letter to me on my 57th.

17 *Beeing Silly* – Playing with love and life…happy words.

18 *Richard* – Janet's birthday letter for my 60th.

19 *The Shadow of Your Wings* – Janet loved to read this with me.

20 *Heads and Tails* – A whimsical piece about our cross-border life.

22 *Tetsubin for Two* – Everyday tensions in a healthy relationship.

23 *A Little Black Box* – A glimpse into Janet's giving nature.

24 *This Old House* – The Toronto home we purchased together.

26 *Christmas 2002* – A Christmas gift to me: *I love it when you…*

27 *A Universal Language* – Janet's joyful heart connected lives.

28 *At the Map Table* – a passive object draws memories of youth.

29 *Gray and Grayer* – Toronto in November, and Hawaii longing.

30 *Tar Baby* – A fascination, connecting words to odd situations.

31 *Everything is Temporary* – A second life for all things tangible.

32 *The Language of Love* – A glimpse into our shorthand dialogue.

To Richard with much love:

A Single Blossom

On the very last day of the longest winter,
A door was finally opened.
We expected a cascade of white-tufted branches:
Instead, a single blossom bloomed.

It was whiter than white
More fragrant than a thousand wild roses
And radiant with its own sense of uniqueness.

A lone bee appeared
Gathering pollen
And touched the secret place
Which would make the cherry grow.

A single cherry:
Redder than red
More succulent than a thousand ripe pears
And as sweet as its fragrance had been.

I touched your shoulder
And in an instant,
A billion luscious memories
A cascade of outrageous feelings
And a profound sense of connectedness
Burst forth.

A rose-breasted grosbeak gently gathered
The nectar from the centre of our hearts,
And we realized that a single blossom would suffice.

Whirlwind Tour

Out of mind but not out of sight
You blow in with
A couple of kisses and hugs,
News of earrings
Paint colours,
A new laptop
And two young boys
Seldom out of Ohio.

You suck up food
And medication,
As a black dog
Conditioned as a puppy
For the ride to "the Koon"
Slips eagerly
Into the back seat
Of your Saab convertible.

Then out of sight but not out of mind,
You leave me to clean the barbeque
And when I look down,
A piece of my heart is missing.

6:50 a.m.
October 19, 1999

Dear Richard,

Happy 57th Birthday! What can I do for you or share with you on this day that would be "excessively fabulous"? I want "excessively fabulous" for you always but also I want other balancing experiences for you as well.

From the beginning, we have been experiencing the golden light together or as a nineteen-year-old artist called it "La Couleur de la Paix". What a wonderful description – "The Color of Peace". Of course, the world tried to distort it royally by leaving out a letter and turning "PAIX" into "PIX".

Perhaps our mission together is to try and help the world return the letter "A" to a very important word. This is not an easy task since we will be compelled to journey constantly to a place of paradox – a place where one finds the opposite of what one thinks she or he is seeking. You are constantly creating a sort of "chaos" in my life as I think I am creating for you also. Where did our seemingly well-ordered lives go? They simply went away, I think, and have been replaced, and will continue to be replaced by a profound sense of hope, and a willingness to go where life leads us.

Of course, we are not helpless in this matter, and are able to chart our own course in terms of choosing how to spend our time, and with whom.

Janet

Beeing Silly

Buzzing through my brain:

Bee is a bee, is a bee, is a bee
Is a bee

To bee or not to bee

A message from the Beeble:
About
Bee coming
                      Bee leaving
Bee ginning (soft "g")
Bee jinning?!?
(definition: a bee sipping a martini)

A love poem
No doubt
Will you bee mine, valentine?
Perhaps my soulbee?
Just like two bees in a bag
Or was that two bees in paradise?
Ah, too bee wildering

Buzzes and bugs (xoxoxoxo)

Richard,

Take note that when you referred to yourself as an "old dog", I didn't know what you were talking about and asked "Is Nel in here?" In other words, you temporarily lost me.

The way I see things, good communication on all levels is still of apramount importance and so when you ask, in fact, "what do you see in me?" the answer is simple: I see you with all of your forthrightness and convolution.

As you have noted lately, we are often thinking exactly the same thoughts and are without a doubt "on the same page". There is no rational explanation for this type of connectedness but one thing I do know is that I feel a profoundly positive sense of attachment to you and that is all that really matters.

So, let's always remember to step back and view our time together as a very precious gift. For, as we both know, there really is no logical explanation for love, and whenever possible, we must rise above the mundane and seek each other's souls.

Love, and love, and love,
Janet

P.S. Thank you for your patience when I am in the depths of a headache and have temporarily lost my joy for living. Whenever you find yourself in a similar predicament, I shall make every effort to treat you with as much TLC as I possibly can.

October 19th, 2002

The Shadow of Your Wings

Just answer yes or no:

Have you been
Living as a dual citizen?
Divorced and sued twice?
Fired once?
Questioned often regarding credit rating?
Accused of and fined
for smuggling an on-consignment carpet?
Answer: *yes*

Have you been
Broken by a horse?
Terrified by a chainsaw?
Ejected by a wooden painting ladder?
Operated on five times?
Traumatized in a serious cycling accident?
Answer: *yes*

And also have you been
Listening to God's Word?
Seeking God's protection?
Assuming stewardship of His land?
Visited by a red-shouldered hawk?
And hidden under the shadow of its wings?
Answer: *yes*

Then you have been hugely blessed
And shall be judged as truly innocent.
Amen

Heads and Tails

They say there's a pot of gold
At the end of the rainbow
But it's actually on the fireplace hearth
And "don't touch it until it's full"

There are pennies saved
And nickels earned
And slippery dimes by the dozen

Quarters cavort with loonies and toonies
And obverse heads begin to roll
As Lincoln
Jefferson
Roosevelt
Washington
Kennedy
And Sacagawea
Commingle with
Her Majesty Queen Elizabeth II

A bald eagle leads a band of
Caribou and beaver
To the top of the pot
Where they force off the lid
With their sheer numbers
And scurry across floors
Like a disturbed nest of cockroaches

Ever-resourceful Sacagawea
Rallies Lewis and Clark
Who lead the frenzied metal masses
To the border
But they are forbidden to cross
For they now number more than
Ten thousand

Ten thousand become ten million
And ten million become a gazillion
Depleting all paper wrapper supplies
And forcing us to our knees
While crying out: "In God We All Must Trust"

TETSUBIN FOR TWO

When "let there be light"
Is cause for disconnection,
And a kitchen knife
Becomes X-Acto,
Frustration turns to anger
As switches and wires
Electrify relationship
Making sparks fly:
And yet laughter
Erupts as quickly,
With the satisfaction
Of a resolution;
And when "read my lips"
Transforms to "thanks"
The ceremony of rejoicing begins,
As the tempest in a teapot
Is put to rest:
Allowing love not only
To be written in stone
But also to be cast in iron:
Forty difficult steps to perfection,
Never missing a single one,
Seeking grace and calm
And austere simplicity
For eternity.

Written for and inspired by Richard Foster who can be very trying and most lovable in the same whisper of breath.

A Little Black Box

I am walking home
from my dental cleaning
when I see a dirt-colored plastic-wrapped envelope
In the street.
I pick it up.
It is from Martha to Alexandra
With a heart cut in it
revealing something black.
I wash the package off
And feel the box
inside the envelope.
Dropped by the postman
how long ago
In his speedy travels
through our neighbourhood.
Is he the smiling young man
in shorts with the prosthetic arm?
Maybe it would be safer
if we picked up and delivered
our own mail…

$1.80 postage
…delivered.

This Old House

The real estate agent's car obscured
The horrific aging of the driveway tarmac;
A coat of gray paint disguised the rot
Of the eaves and soffits;
Peeling wallpaper concealed water stains,
The kitchen grease and blocked drain went unnoticed,
But the Corian countertop and white tile floor
Revealed large telltale cracks.

Twenty-year-old carpeting was marred by a dirty bare spot
Where a percussionist had practiced very long ago;
Heavy draperies concealed a lifeless garden
Devoid of even a healthy weed;
There was no bidding war
And so armed with the almost-blind energy of our love
We committed to the transformation.

Old wallpaper, carpeting, dusty blinds
And cock-eyed bifold doors
Found a new home in the dumpster,
While cork and hardwood
Created a warm and friendly ambience;
A young friend christened our abode "The Happy House"
And a former Jesuit priest blessed our life together.

At every turn there was struggle and strife
And sleepless nights over leaking roofs and skylights,
Tearful encounters of misunderstanding
And lack of communication;
Duct work that was never in the right place,
Inadequate telephone and cable wiring,
And sewer flies that seemed relentless.

Unnecessary lies and deception were encountered,
And favours that were not:
Even the exterior paint was altered by the overly zealous,
Creating a tri-coloured nightmare;
Unexpected blockers were the norm;
Anything that went "well" was suspect.

We tried to see our renovation problems as challenges,
Still our hair turned grayer and got thinner,
Our joints became stiffer and our teeth disintegrated,
But our house continued to fill with light
And the joy of birthdays and baby showers
And a spiritual commitment
To continue towards the light;

Acknowledging the wonder of the red-shouldered hawk
Perched among the glowing greenery of the oaks and maples;
The magnificence of the monarch butterfly
Hovering over the kitchen skylight,
The love of friends and family,
And the mysterious ways of an all-powerful God
Who is perpetually moving us ever-nearer to the day
When we shall be called to dwell in His house forever.

The Shadow of Your Wings

CHRISTMAS 2002

I loved it when you:

Said: "hey Janet, guess what...I found my address book."

Laughed when I suggested that if you bought "short" clothing then you could have them lengthened.

Listened when I was bitching about the Xmas party.

Rubbed my back and I could feel your touch for a long time afterwards.

Thanked me for helping you with your turkey dinner.

Didn't go crazy when I had to do an "extra good" job cleaning the new oven.

Stayed up late with me until Laura was safely home.

Sent me an E.S.P. message about wanting Fish and Chips for supper.

Thought that buying small gold boxes of truffles from the Chocolate Messenger was a good idea.

Admitted that watching the ultra-violent "We Were Solders" was not great for your psyche.

Decided to take the helicopter into the resort on St. Lucia.

Tried to deal rationally with the hot tub next door sticking out into the ravine.

A Universal Language

As we are exiting from Kale
Our very favorite vegetarian restaurant,
A young woman with a baby carriage in front
and a toddler behind her
is struggling down the steps.
She turns to apologize for blocking our way.
She has limited English vocabulary
but seems to understand our message:
No rush, don't hurry… it's ok
I try to gently steady the toddler in front of me
and finally, we are all safely on the sidewalk.
The mother and daughter walk away
but the child continues to turn around
To see me.
I blow a kiss in her direction
and she blows one back.
The mother does the same.
My day is complete.

AT THE MAP TABLE

We are eating asparagus
and red-pepper quiche
And a green salad with assorted fruit
Waiting for our tea to finish steeping
when I notice a map above our table –
A National Geographic map of the British Isles.
I realize that my experience consists of
London, Heathrow airport, Devon
and the white cliffs of Dover
where so many years ago
a ferry crossed the English Channel to France
With me on it.

My luncheon companion would like to visit Scotland
In the summertime.

GRAY AND GRAYER

Is everything gray?

The car is gray
The driveway is gray
The walkway is gray
The roadway is gray
The house across the street is gray
The entire sky is precisely the same gray.

After a gray shower
With gray water
I notice my black Hawaii
shirt with the bleached stains
and rhinestones
depicting gray palm trees:
Delineating gray
And I remember the light
and the moist, warm air
The sense of coming home
And I long for that reward.

My childhood watercolour
palette flashes in my brain
Light gray and dark gray:
Perhaps there is a fleeting ray of
hope for this delightful day.

TAR BABY

In
India,
A dog falls into a tar pit.
He is found sticking to the roadway.

In
Ohio,
I step out of our car
Wearing brand new Nike running shoes
I am sticking to the roadway.

In
Oberlin,
I enter the art gallery
To find a washroom
I am sticking to the floor.

In
Twinsburg,
Goo-Gone goes deep into tread
Turns brown and spreads onto
Paper towel and a microfiber cloth.
I am sticking to the task at hand.

In the
laundry
room,
I do not throw the cloth away
but put it in the washing machine.
I turn back my cream-coloured sheets
And find a brownish black sticky speck.

In the
present,
I think about those, tarred and feathered.
The dog rescued by animal lovers
Knowing that their lives,
like mine were permanently changed
For I am still sticking to my story.

Everything is Temporary

Everything is temporary.
Take a picture of it.

Almost gone to landfill
I took it apart –
Then I put it back together

One zipper broken
Half of a strap missing

I could have fixed the zipper
And replaced the missing strap
Anyone could do that –

Well, almost anyone.

But no one will be able to repeat
What I have done without considerable
Difficulty

My victory!
What is that on the floor?
Just random pieces at the moment
And a pair of scissors

Now it works perfectly.

THE LANGUAGE OF LOVE

After fifteen years, we are at liberty to communicate in "secret code"
If you said this to me in the dark, I would know it was you....

Who are you tickin' to...	means	To whom are you talking?
This is an excellent brew if I do say so myself ...	means	Praise God for green juice
Walking to Seattle ...	means	How non-flyers get to Hawaii
Danke schon bitte ... (shane) (beater)	means	Thank you
Bonjour ...	means	good morning
See you in the matin ...	means	good night
Tally-ho, loveydoo ...	means	steady on, my love
Manana ...	means	see you tomorrow
Where are you now? ...	means	How much longer until you are home?
Just an FYI ...	means	I would like to point something out without angering of offending you.
Get over it ...	means	Let it go... move on.
Life is too short ...	means	Don't intellectualize or overthink that subject, event, occurrence

Let's go off together, just you and me …	means	*An isolating snowstorm when going out is dangerous.*
Green cemetery …	means	-black walnut ice cream -an Amish man with nine children -property where hawks soar -wicker baskets -leaving a legacy -land next to the Grand River -a resting place for displaced ashes -not the Mount Pleasant cemetery

EVERYDAY CONVERSATIONS

The majority of our eighteen-year life together was grounded by our home in Toronto, and a daily life together there that settled into a rhythm that revolved around a very active teenage daughter, pets, mothers in their 80s and 90s, family gatherings, new grandchildren – and of course, our many vacation adventures together, which Janet enjoyed referring to as "excessively fabulous." There were long stretches of our Toronto life when my Ohio-based business required me to do weekly commutes to Cleveland. In hindsight I can see that those times actually kept our conversations deeper and more active than most married couples experience when in the presence of one another continuously, day-to-day.

In 2000, Janet and I purchased a home together in Bennington Heights, Toronto, an area of the city where Janet had spent her entire life, and we maintained that home together until 2016 when we purchased a home in Ohio located in Moreland Hills. Janet did a great deal of writing throughout this period of our lives together, some of which I've compiled in this book.

My selection of Janet's writings in this chapter covers a wide range of personal experiences, observations, reflections, humor and enduring faith. Janet might call it a collage. It includes pieces from when we lived in Ohio fighting cancer, and earlier pieces from before we met that she chose to share with me.

36 *Keep It Simple* – Juxtapositions of elements, expressions.

38 *A Victorian House is not a Home* – A horrid B&B experience.

40 *A Call from Brad Pitt* – Janet and a telemarketer.

41 *Ode to Cents* – Lamenting the loss of the Canadian penny.

42 *God Save the Queen* – Reflecting back in time with Queen E.

43 *In All the Wrong Places* – Early years, searching for Christ.

44 *All About the AGO (Dear Dan)* – A kind gift thwarted.

46 *The Meeting Place* – An encounter from prior teaching days.

48 *Aiden* – Recognizing a former student – lost potential.

49 *Invest in Something Wonderful* – Journal entry – on giving.

50 *Girl Watcher* – An observation turns back time to age fourteen.

51 *Left Hand Confronts Right Hand* – Regarding a broken wrist.

52 *Dear Nancy* – Reflects about my first wife after memorial.

54 *Kathy* – What's known and loved about cousin Kathy.

56 *i'm my mom's kid* – A conversation in a school hallway.

58 *Her Body is Her Song* – A restaurant waitress observed.

59 *Thunder Rolls* – Trash collection day, neighbor nightmare.

60 *24 Hour Notice Required* – Creative humor. Death and dying.

KEEP IT SIMPLE

I have a new password
It is: keep it simple

And so, on the 19th of December
I made a big pot of chicken stew
(which only took 3 days to make)
And no-sugar homemade blueberry biscuits
(which James loved)
We ordered three pizzas
from Pizza Pizza
and they were placed on the boxes
on our walnut Dutch colony table.
After a pinecone hunt,
a tree-decorating event on the deck,
a gift exchange
and a Rice Krispies icing event
featuring gum drops, red & green M&M's
Jelly beans, Cadbury eggs, Twister Pulls,
and icing glue
(which turned out to be a definite hit)
we built a crazy fort
and then it was time to clean up.
Pizza boxes headed for the garbage
leaving a distinct white mark on the
walnut Dutch colony table circa 1860.
On to the next celebration
deal with it later.

Rebound One:
Later arrives & internet recommends
Toothpaste & mayonnaise & ashes
One spot cleaned & waxed,
remove mats… 3 more spots.
Deal with later.

Rebound Two:
Toothpaste, mayo, wood ashes
Wax
Polish
table almost like new ("patina" of marks)
and I am relieved
that I was able to
Keep It Simple
Keep It Simple

A Victorian House is not a Home

*"Enter and be welcomed by the fabulous front door
with original rich oak trim and extensive leaded
stained glass windows throughout"*
                              (In the B&B owners' words)

The host cautiously tiptoes in slippers
Afraid he might spill a drop of coffee,
And feels silly asking us to remove our sandals
Exposing our smelly, naked feet,
While our hostess sits primly at her computer
Arranging a picture-perfect environment
According to Martha Stewart.

Suddenly a two-year-old materializes,
Knocking over meticulously arranged Depression glass,
Throwing up on the pristine white bedcovering
And tarnishing the towels.

Immediately and without a trial
The tot is convicted of vandalism
And transported to Auschwitz.

Breakfast arrives as a calculated arrangement of food bits
Which we feel compelled to eat
And we try to use muffled laughter to de-stress
In the hope that our sweaty hands, feet and armpits
Will not be discovered.

After breakfast, I retrieve my white linen napkin
Used to cover up the single drop of coffee
And recall the words "I see you have already made a mess",
Unfold it graciously,
And without shame
Wipe off my sweaty, naked feet.

Amen

A Call from Brad Pitt

The phone rings
I put my thoughts away
And am prepared
To listen, listen, listen
While a voice from Calcutta
Expounds about this and that,
With me interjecting, this and that
To keep the monologue in line
As he asks me for my name
And I say:
I will tell you mine
If you tell me yours
And so, I do and he does:

"Janet from Toronto"

    "I am Joe Black from New York"

        End of Conversation.

ODE TO CENTS

There was a time
When one hundred Canadian cents
Made one dollar
But now no dollar makes cents.

Rounding up or down is the case
$19.95 becomes $20.00
$29.95 becomes $30.00
All bargains have disappeared.

No more standing
In front of the till
Waiting to count the copper change,
Only nickel, silver, brass, bronze
And plastic will go back in your pocketbook

Yes, plastic.
Imagine plastic bills in your wallet or purse
All shiny and bright
With a little coating of some toxic material
Just like most paper receipts
Now injurious to our health

Nothing sacred
Nothing immortal
As kings and queens die
And popes retire.
The "penny" too, long gone
Along with all trusty sayings.
All sense replaced by nonsense.

All nonsense replaced by no cents.

GOD SAVE THE QUEEN

When I was six I broke my arm
While rough-housing with my brother
Then I went to school and sang:

God save our gracious **Queen**!
Long live our noble **Queen**!
God save the **Queen**!
Send her victorious,
Happy and glorious,
Long to reign over us:
God save the **Queen**!

Now I am sixty-seven and I have broken my arm
While roller skating in the company of my husband,
son and granddaughter.
I am now in my bed reminiscing and singing:

God save our gracious **Queen**!
Long live our noble **Queen**!
God save the **Queen**!
Send her victorious,
Happy and glorious,
God save the **Queen**!

Queen Elizabeth The Second was ninety years old yesterday.
My prayerful song seems to have worked.
But while drinking two cups of organic jasmine tea in her honour
I was wondering if the Queen of England has ever broken her arm.

IN ALL THE WRONG PLACES

On a long-ago trip to Washington, D.C.
I started my search for Christ
In all the wrong places.

Treadmills, gristmills, silos and barns.
Traffic noises and games and
Stalactites
Did not lead me to God.

The bleating of a spring lamb
in a near-silent valley
Did not secure my path,

A sculpture called "Awakening"
led me to Christ's crucifixion
But not to Resurrection or Ascension
or Second Coming.

The thought of Christ blessing me
And then exiting while in the process
Leaving me alone in my grief
But with a promise of joy to follow,
is totally Awesome.

For now I see the Ruler of all
Upon His throne
Taking care of all universal business
And... earthly... business
And at the same time
Taking care of me.

Amen

All About the AGO

Dear Dan
Thanks for reminding me
In October that I took out a
membership to the AGO,
thinking that it was the ROM.
Eventually I realized that
the museum had turned into
the Art Gallery – the famous
architectural art gallery
of the renowned Frank Gehry
born and bred in Toronto but
soon to move to L.A. USA.
Instead of doing something for me,
I would do something for Richard:
Namely go to the Art Gallery many times
To explore the new architecture:
The melding of old and new
        past and present
And marvel at the glorious compromise.

The Best Laid Plans

Oct. 4
First came the face peel
for precancerous spots
No light for two days
And no sun for six more
70 sunblock forever.

Nov. 4
Indian summer arrived
On exactly the 4th of November
The forces of evil were lurking
Richard headed north to close up the cottage
He was being very careful
Sincc he was all alone

Richard was on the ladder
that had a propensity for falling over.
It was a beautiful day.
He was being very careful.

Richard went down
The rough ground came up
And his ankle once intact was history
(I will spare you the details)

Dec. 4
A nasty flu moves in
while Richard is immobilized
Then he has two teeth removed
which calls for antibiotics
and more pain killers and antihistamines
And Tylenol and you name it …

In Richard's own words: I am a wreck.

So: We haven't been to visit the
"revised" version of the AGO
but with so many drugs in his system,
Richard might actually enjoy the art
(He is already having weird hallucinatory dreams)

Never mind the Frank Gehry architecture!

THE MEETING PLACE

As I trudged through slush and snow
Past a frozen dead pigeon,
I saw an old lady in black;
Her eyes met mine,
And we went to a common place:
Grace Street School
Room 224
Where I taught
And she had swept and dusted

A few words moved us
Through many years:
I had married,
She had lost her husband;
Her family were young people,
"You know, not the same."
"Merry Christmas", she said quietly
As I boarded the streetcar

In her day
She would pick up pins
One by one
And hand them to me:
The new staff
Swept blocks and puzzle pieces
Out to the hall
Awaiting the trash bin.

My rose was bruised
But still alive,
Nostalgia filled the air.

Santa Claus was riding the subway;
Really, it was really him.
He had the most amazing
Sparkling blue eyes:
Only the red suit was missing.

All had not ended:
A last lunch perhaps,
A non-existent formal good-bye
And yet another new beginning.

Aiden

I cannot read your name tag
But I know, I know you
I wait for you to turn
And I am right
I remember a very young boy
In an After-Four class
Always strangely wonderful
Now a Loblaws cashier
You ring up my
Tomatoes and peameal bacon:
  $13.13 change
It is Sunday
And I *think:* God numbers.
You *say:* These are very lucky numbers.
I say: Yes, I know.
I leave with my two items
And one question: What else will you think and do
When *you* leave this place.

    You touch my food

Christmas Day 2011

INVEST IN SOMETHING WONDERFUL

*We have been blessed with six World Vision children.
(Every month two hundred and ten dollars is automatically
removed from our bank account).*

They have names and they live on planet earth and require
water, food, clothing, love and spiritual sustenance just
like the rest of us. On occasion, I send them birthday cards,
magic markers, and calculators, and words describing my life
without sounding pompous or overbearing. It is difficult,
since I seem to have so much, and they so little, but it is
actually the other way around. They are richer, and I am
essentially poorer. Each day they must struggle to live
and grow and co-operate with each other in order to survive.
I must go to the gym, and the drug store, and the supermarket,
and the big box vendor for light bulbs. I visit a Halfway House
delivering leftover party food, but I do not get out of the car.
Only the smell of tipped-over salad dressing remains.
I have health insurance to pay for my doctor to take my
blood pressure, and weigh me, and tell me that I need a calcium
supplement… two more PAP tests in my lifetime … and a bone
density test, along with a colonoscopy and a flu shot. If I lived
in Africa in a small village, none of these "miracle" preventatives
would be available. I would be born, live and die just like everyone
else. Please don't get me wrong – I am grateful for many of the
options presented to me, but I know that there is more to life then
I have dared to explore. Keeping my hands clean seems
unconscionable.

I know I can do more.

Girl Watcher

We find our spot in the audience
To the far left of the band
Behind the porta potty
and in front of the security fence,
uphill from the sound and smell
of the milling crowd and fried sausages.

She appears.
A young woman in a pink strapless blouse
and a long flowing ecru skirt with a perfectly
matching ecru-suede fringed handbag
over her shoulder.

Old-fashioned in a bohemian sort of way
She stands as still as a Great Blue Heron
Stalking a fish
Is she intent on gaining the favor of the lead singer,
or is she the ex-girlfriend of the drummer?
Perhaps the former lover of the saxophone player?

And I remember early days on the park bench
Watching you play tennis with a mutual friend
Being asked to play
And the music of Chicago plays in my head.
It seems like yesterday.

And now I'm just a girlwatcher
But she is suddenly gone.
We do not see her walk or fly away
The band begins to play a song:
just a ...   just a girl watcher.

LEFT HAND CONFRONTS RIGHT HAND

It took an entire week for the left hand to pose the question:
"What are you doing?"
The right hand responded:
"Nothing."
"I've noticed," said the left hand.
"You are no longer a leader, supporter and best Friend,
I must comb hair, brush teeth, apply deodorant,
pull up pants, wash feet and put on decompression stockings,
all by myself,
In the kitchen, you pass me a knife, the cup, the spoon,
knowing that I am next to useless
with all pots, pans, utensils and dishes.
In the garden, I must deal with the weeds and dirt – alone.
I look to you for help and the most you can do
is wiggle your fingers at me
Without you, I am afraid to drive the car or walk down stairs."
"So, what's up?"
"Nothing," says the right hand.

Sunday September 21, 2014

Dear Nancy

I am awakened at 6:14 a.m.
by a clap of thunder --
It has been a fitful night.
Your memorial service is next Sunday
but has been announced on Facebook as being today.

Our paths have crossed
for the last sixteen years
even though we have never formally met.

I know about cats on gurneys,
A pet store and financial issues,
and even a time removing promotional pennies from magazines.
You had an aunt Etta whose rocking chair is at the cottage.
A father named Austin
and a sister Cathy.

After surviving non-Hodgkin's lymphoma,
you married my husband a second time
at the site overlooking Kalaupapa in Hawaii.
I have been there many times –
once with flower petals strewn on the ground.
You lived at Dixie Maru
where turkeys flourish –
I lived there too.

When a serious heart condition
threatened your existence
I prayed for you.
When I was diagnosed with cancer
you prayed for me.

I was in Toronto
on the 23rd of December
as you were struggling
to live and die with a brain tumor.
I like to think a candle eased your passage home.

And here I stand
honouring you
in the company of family and friends,
knowing that someday
we will meet in God's garden:
You will be feeding all of the animals.
I will be watering all of the plants.
And we will both be eating an apple
from one of your trees –
to make sure that the apples are good enough
to feed to the horses.

KATHY

I think of you as I transfer laundry
From washing machine to dryer:
>*Shaken sheets do dry better.*

Wooden cutting boards rule
Over plastic and glass:
>*Steel blades on wood sound kinder.*

You believe in the healing power
Of organic cider vinegar and virgin olive oil:
>*Measured doses are essential.*

Falling in the water and surviving the tornado
Are part of your experience:
>*A lifejacket is a must.*

Strength comes from walks in the company
Of moss and rock and babbling brook:
>*All three enhance your spirit.*

Allergic to cats and dogs cause you grief
But undaunted by mice:
>*An asset at the cottage.*

Your blood must be monitored
For signs of change:
>*The ups and downs are draining.*

You enjoy winning at Chinese Checkers
And shuffleboard too:
>*The victory hug is sweet.*

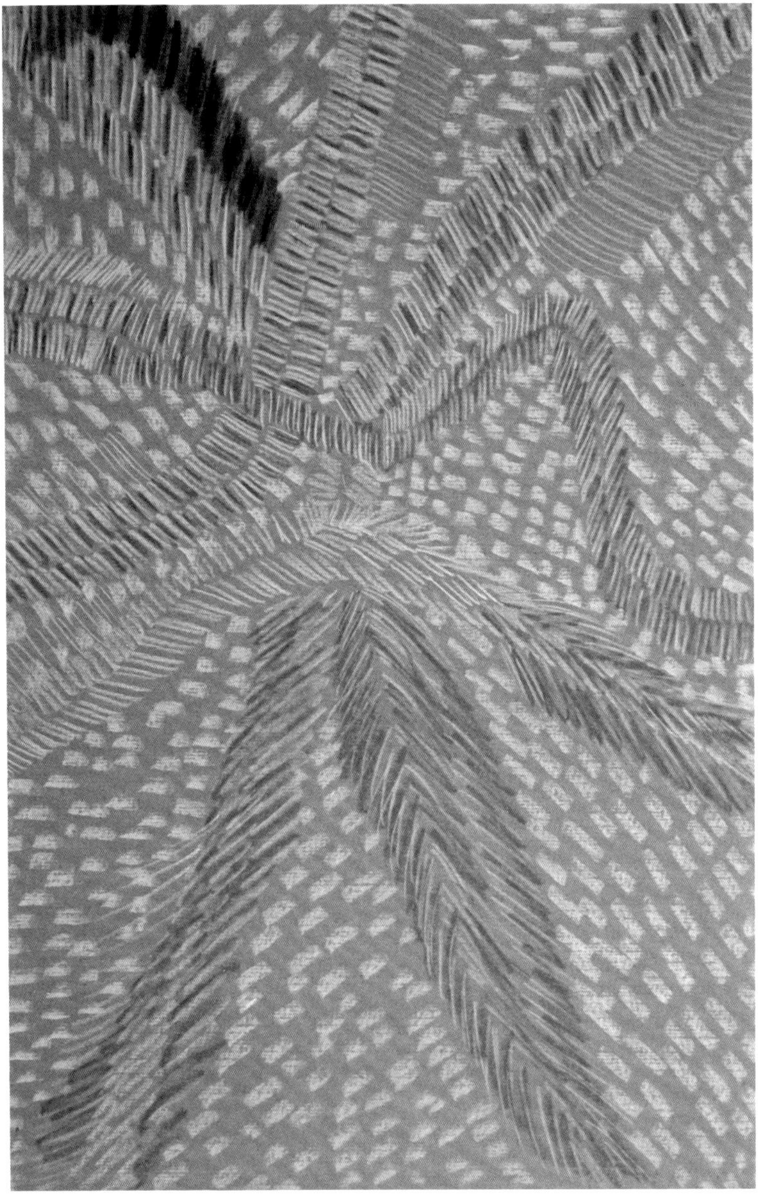

I'M MY MOM'S KID

Sometimes my mom thinks
that i'm just a noisy kid
and that red licorice gets me crazy
but that's all right
'cause i'm my mom's kid

Some mornings i'm very tired
i don't want to get dressed
get in the car
and go to daycare
but i do it anyway
'cause i'm my mom's kid

One day i was lying
in the doorway
of my mom's classroom
down the hall
from where i go every day
she was talking to another mom
about scarecrows and beanbags
and other important stuff
i listened as i lay
in the dust and the millipedes
'cause i'm my mom's kid

I can get a hug
as i pass by
to go to kindergarten
or at lunch time
or one or two after school
if i know the right time to ask
i don't get reminded
about where i'm supposed to be
or what i'm supposed to be doing
once i even got a hug
without asking for it
'cause i'm my mom's kid

I know that most stories
are supposed to have a happy ending
but this story doesn't end
'cause i will always be my mom's kid

HER BODY IS HER SONG

Her body is her song
But, beauty doesn't last
I know because I've been there
It is all in the past.
Her stance
Her hair beyond compare
No tattoos, scar or blemish
She runs with those
Whose lives expose
The shallowness of drink.
She knows it all and will not fail
To listen to what you think.
She's coming up with zeroes
The money flows with tips galore.
She's bought into the game
And feels no shame.

But in her eyes and hug and smile
I see a God so great
Creator, lover, doer, carer
I know it's not too late
For *heart felt Beauty* is her true song
And I pray that the next verse
Will expose your spirit and your soul
And allow her to rehearse
An eternal song
Of love with you.

Thunder Rolls

A steamy summer night in April
brings lightning thunder and deluge

car with music blaring arrives on scene
4:54 a.m.

enormous garbage can thunders to the curb

lid slams thunder rolls lid slams
5:10 a.m.

robins start up on the branch touching my window
God's thunder rolls off to another street

Did I just open the front door in my underwear
with a wad of compression bandage on my right arm
and scream an obscenity?

Or did I wait patiently with finger on iPad
for relative calm to return?

robins fly off to another tree
5:57 a.m.

train whistle beckons on opposite side of Route 91
6:13 a.m.

It must be another Tuesday morning.

24 Hour Notice Required

I have a simple request:
In case of an emergency
Or a sudden change of heart,
Please give me
Twenty-four hour notice.

I do not adjust well
To sudden changes:
Dying instantly is my dread,
Should my days be numbered,
Please throw in an extra one
For good measure.

All I want is the chance
To say good-bye
And to make sure
That no dirty laundry
Is left behind.

Perhaps a lifetime
Of half-finished projects
Could be resolved,
Or our Will finally written,
Or the potted Christmas evergreen
Put to rest:
At least the gerbils could be fed.

My parents were both
Noble enough
To die on Friday:
Everyone went back to work
On Monday.
I say Protestant Work Ethic
Be damned.
A perfectly good weekend
Should not be spent
In mourning.

Some people ask
For one more birthday
Or one more Spring,
Simply remember
My honest request:
Please give me

NATURE CONVERSATIONS

When I entered Janet's home for the first time I was taken by the amount of plants she had throughout, including a lime tree she'd been growing in her family room for more than twenty years. Each plant had a story, grown from cuttings with emotional connections – plants grown by her grandmother, her mother, or friends. Janet and I were a gardening team from the very beginning. Gardening and all things in nature was a wonderfully creative and spiritual connection for us. We worked hard together in our Toronto, Molokai and Ohio gardens, designing, planting and maintaining them as well as rebuilding and nurturing the soil. Although Janet had only one garden season at our Ohio home, she loved every moment of it, touching every leaf, every stem, every flower petal. Nurturing every vegetable sprout, lovingly transferring her energy, and having spirit conversation with every form of life, light and shadow in her garden. It was a season of continuously unfolding gifts, pure joy of God's visible presence from March through November. A Toronto girl comfortable with big city life, Janet became a lover of Ohio and its parks, hiking trails, nature sanctuaries and wildlife – especially the great blue heron rookeries. Often she would say, "Let's take a walk…take me somewhere I've never been before."

---

64   *A Hyacinth Saved by a Dove* – Sisters experience kind heart.

65   *Good Morning Miss Dove* – Remembering a favorite teacher.

66   *April the 22nd, 2002: Sprinter* – Spring becomes winter.

67   *In Honour of Moth Worms* – A battle of wits.

68   *Counting My Crocuses* – A journal story of a gardening battle.

71   *Apples from an Orange Tree* – "Living hedges" connections.

72   *Outside In* – A past moment reflected, treasured with humor.

74   *Original Sin* – Garden life…an analogy.

76   *The Bug from Hell* – An assassin bug moment.

78   *Blue Day For a Spruce* – An employee ax job.

79   *Birds in My Life* – Moments remembered.

82   *Cutting Roses on a Summer Morning* – A city moment.

83   *On the Wane* – Janet loved words, and played with them.

84   *Hefty OneZip* – Nature invents solutions, imagination plays.

85   *Watching Time Pass* – A spiritual moment with nature.

86   *A Reason for Gardenphobia* – In memory of Annabelle.

89   *Odds and Ends* – Juxtaposition of disparate elements.

90   *Black Coffee* – Will our holly bush accept almond milk?

91   *For Every Action* – A story of a chipmunk and a geranium.

A Hyacinth Saved by a Dove

On a cold wintery afternoon …
long, long ago …
a child of six or seven
came into possession
of a Hyacinth in blossom

She arrived at her sister's classroom …
a magical place …
where the teacher
took pity on the naked plant
and wrapped it snugly
for its homeward journey

Never forgetting the experience …
and profoundly impressed …
the two sisters
eventually became teachers
aspiring always to do the same

GOOD MORNING MISS DOVE

I have often wondered if the Miss Dove in the movie was *My Miss Dove.*

My Miss Dove fed us hard tack and molasses, allowed us to get porcupine quills stuck in our sweaters, and cactus spines in our fingers. She seated us next to butterfly chrysalises that hatched in the spring after being sprayed with a watery mist for weeks. And she had me draw an elf picture for the square window in the classroom door. And taught me to spell "Cristmas'"with an "H" when my caroling toilet paper roll angel had forgotten how.

After two years I had completed three years of school, having learned much about the world from butterflies to Vikings, to (Norse) fiords, and also about the necessity of protecting a hyacinth from cold winds on wintery days.

April the Twenty-Second
Two Thousand Two

Surprise! Sprinter has returned,
Stunning a bedraggled raccoon
As he passes by the back door
In midday.

Tiny flowers shiver
Beneath an icy blanket
Unaccustomed to the roller coaster ride.

My head and I recognize the pattern
After the fact.
Now I understand why
A major thread count is necessary:

Not under the duvet
But fully reclining in my green leather chair,
Sipping medicinal Pepsi
Trying to absorb the extra-strength Tylenol
So sleep will come.

God feels my pain and mercifully
Eliminates the cleaning woman
And vacuum cleaner noises from the agenda.

   Let it snow,
    Let it snow,
     Let it snow, I say.

In Honour of Moth Worms

Inside the steamer trunk,
Underneath the white paper,
Beside the painted spaghetti,
    That's where I found the skeletal remains.

First my woolly underwear,
Next my Holt Renfrew skirt,
Then my cashmere sweater,
All remorselessly attacked.
  Outrage, acceptance, rationalisation, I experienced them all.

If I don't give away,
Sell or ragbag items unworn,
Not to worry;
Eventually they will be eaten up:
  A rather slow way to reduce inventory but ultimately effective.

I think they do it
In broad daylight,
But you never see them.
Only the evidence remains;
In one side…out the other,
They perform the unmentionable.
    No one talks about them; we are not supposed to;
        we all wage a silent war.

Counting My Crocuses

Last autumn, contrary to my better judgment, I planted seventy-five crocus bulbs. My sister had received them as a free gift with her very first online order of tulip bulbs from British Columbia. She had no place to plant them, she claimed, and so asked me if I would like to take them. And so, I popped them into the ground as deeply as I felt I could, given the size of the bulb, to protect them from squirrels and winter thaws.

Immediately our family of black squirrels went insane with excitement and proceeded to methodically dig, dig, dig, and replant their treasure trove of bulbs as I frantically back-filled their holes, made threatening noises and chased them away whenever I could.

One November day, I was about to get into the car to leave for Ohio, when I noticed several unearthed bulbs that needed my attention. As my husband waited patiently in the driver's seat, I speedily replanted the bulbs and dashed down the stairs to the tap on the side of the house to wash my hands before breathlessly settling in the passenger's seat.

Throughout my six week absence, I often imagined the squirrels having rousing get-togethers in my crocus bed as they challenged one another regarding the digging up of the most bulbs.

When I returned in January to naked, frozen ground, unearthed bulbs were visible. For a week or so, I didn't know what to do but finally decided to mound a 30-litre bag of potting soil over the top of the area.

The winter advanced as the warmest, most snowless and most random in all of history.

I recalled a year when I had planted one hundred daffodil bulbs and only one had come up. According to a newspaper article by Fred Dale, I was not alone due to all the freezing and thawing that had occurred that particular February.

While I had been expecting to wander "lonely as a cloud, o'er vales and hills", and see "A host of golden daffodils" as William Wordsworth and his sister Dorothy had in 1802, I was, instead, disappointed and sorely dismayed.

And now, in the middle of March, unseasonable 70 to 80 degree temperatures are forcing bulbs of all sorts but especially the early crocuses. Some are coming up alone in odd locations, and as I walk through the neighborhood, I imagine that many of the larger and more colorful specimens are actually those planted originally by *my* hand in *my* crocus bed.

Anyway, the crocus season is very short, and I am counting my crocuses as they hatch, so to speak, and loving every minute of it.

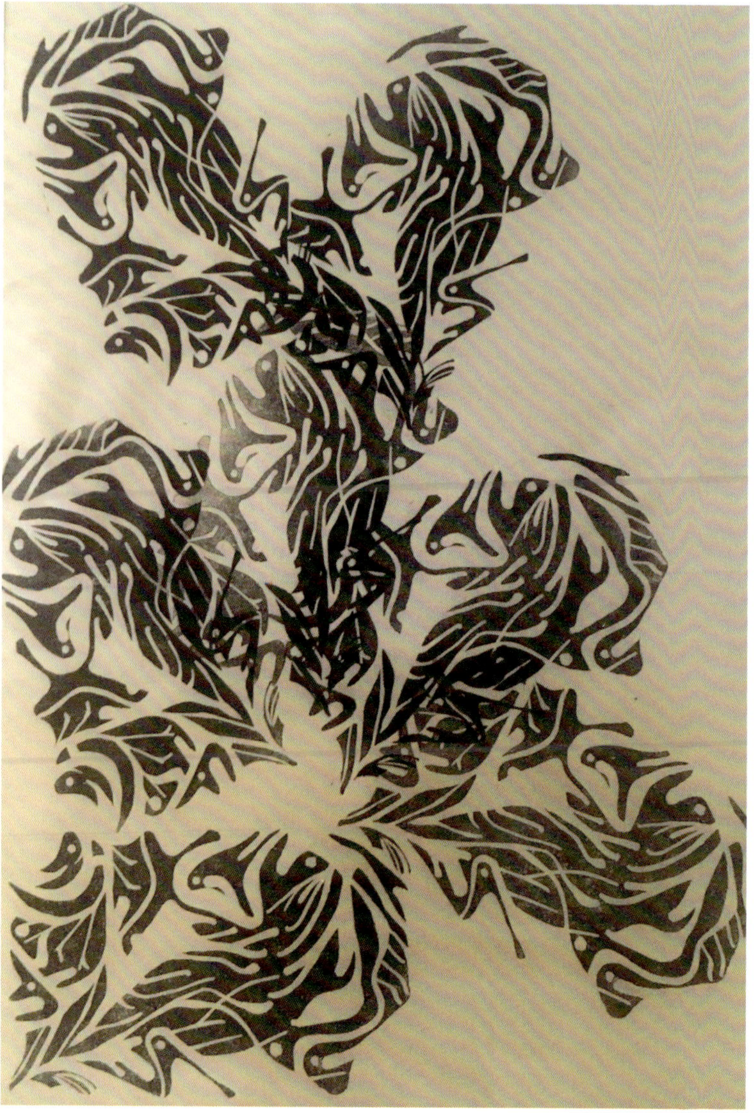

APPLES FROM AN ORANGE TREE

While walking from Hudson Ohio
To Seattle Washington
I stumble upon large green brain-like balls
And tentatively pick one up
Are they poisonous?
I carry them as far as I can get
Before my driver picks me up
Just past the St. Mary's cemetery
I am taken to the Woodlands
Where I Google "large green balls"
Which leads me to the Osage Orange Tree
And suddenly I am visited by pioneers
Planting living hedges to keep the deer out
And their cows and pigs in
And Osage Indians that I want to know about
And spider repellant and thorny Carissa plants
Along the driveway on Molokai
Planted by new millennium pioneers
To protect their citrus grove
From thirteen thousand magnificant
But uninvited invaders
As we see how history repeats itself
And how hedge apples can grow on orange trees

"Horse high but strong & hog tight"

OUTSIDE IN

It was just
a garden-variety spider
about two shrieks
from leg tip to leg tip,
Sitting in the centre
acting as the hub
of the orb.

I knew that the new sunroof
would do more than
allow rain to soak the upholstery.

We both laughed
when we saw it
and didn't have
the heart to destroy.

Adam sat
in the front seat
without his booster
in order to accommodate
this travelling treasure.

I drove slowly
and checked for spiders
in the rear-view mirror
at every corner.

Who would have imagined
that spiders
are really
very agreeable
backseat drivers?

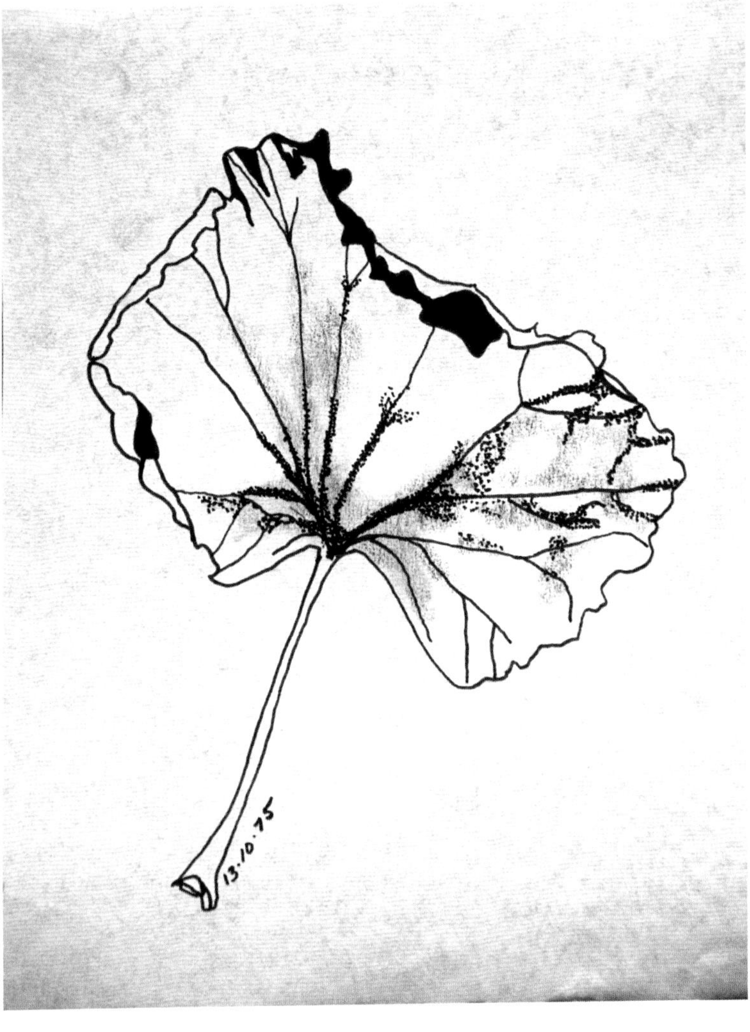
13.10.75

ORIGINAL SIN

In the original garden
there were two trees:
the Tree of Life
and the Tree of Knowledge.

(Perhaps both are still there
since God had the sense
to evict all forms of human life
before it was too late.)

In the neighbour's garden
There were two trees:
A Bloodgood Japanese Maple
And a Dwarf Japanese Cutleaf Maple.

(Both are now gone
since she did not have the sense
to evict all forms of human life
before it was too late.)

In my garden
There are two trees:
A Bloodgood Japanese Maple
And a Dwarf Japanese Cutleaf Maple.

(Both contribute in their own way:
Bloodgood bears its own fruit
While Cutleaf supports the growth
of other plants.)

I do not wish to
Evict all forms of human life
From my garden,
And so I must endure
Children with swords
Who stand on my rock
And slash at my tree.

Certainly times haven't changed much
But it is not my place to play God.

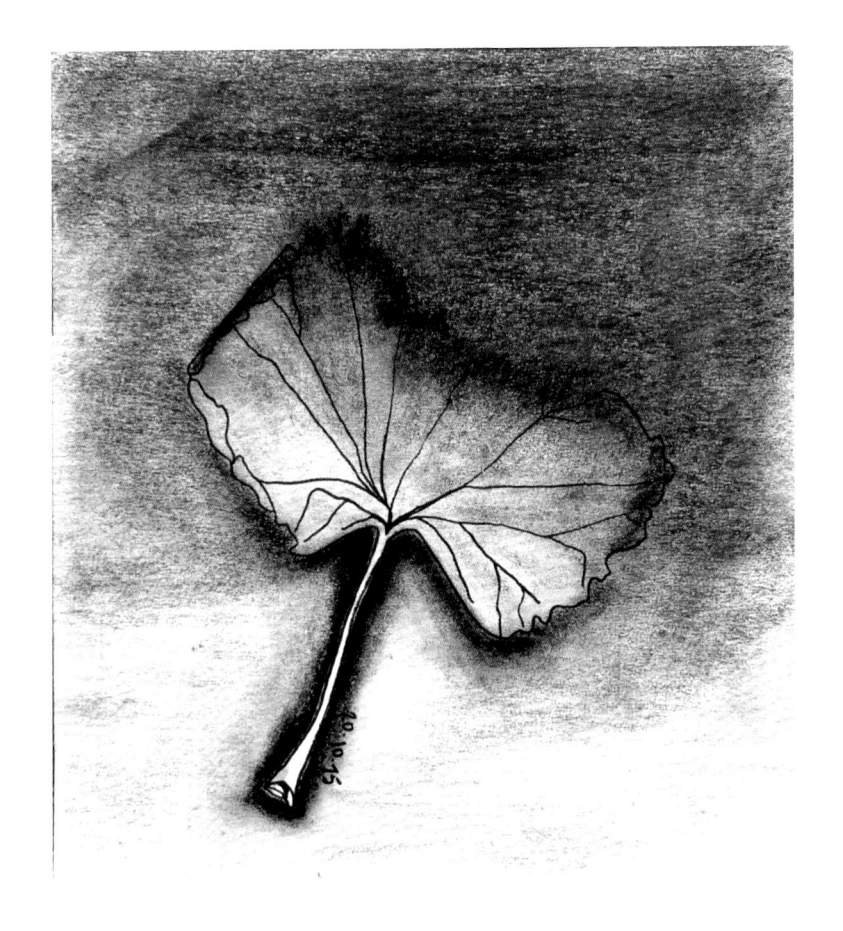

The Bug from Hell

I am sitting in my green chair
watching Will Galloway's chickens
eating insects in her garden on YouTube.
When a beetle crashes into my picture window
on the inside of the glass.

I capture it in a French jam jar
wondering all the while
just what kind of beetle
it could be and where it came from.

The wood pile comes to mind
And I fear woodboring insects
that may infest my home foundation
leaving sawdust as a calling card.

Then I wait... an answer:

My 31-year-old son and his family arrive for a visit
and the bug in the jar is a definite hit
with the grandchildren.

"What do you think it is", I ask?
And my son promptly states:
"An assassin bug".
I laugh and say: "You should know"

as I remember a six-year-old insect lover
asking his mother
if he should touch a black beetle in the house
and being told: "sure, why not"
and getting stung by a venomous bite
which caused uncontrollable tears
and anger that could only be assuaged
by flushing the very very nasty bug
down the toilet.

BLUE DAY FOR A SPRUCE

There is something very sad
About a felled tree,
One must always wonder why:
Firewood?
Safety?
Disease?
Man's desire to take control?
How brave
With saw in hand
When in a single breath
The deed is done.
Twenty years of growth
In sun, wind, rain and snow
Erased forever.
Chop, chop,
Into the dumpster
Without remorse.
Fence and building
Are looking bare
Without the gentle blue presence.
Forget the whys and wherefores
For who shall notice by tomorrow?
Only know this:
There is something very sad
About a felled tree.

Birds in My Life

I know the names of more birds than most
but not the seventeen varieties of warblers
that fly through our ravine every spring.

When you mention the word dove
I return to a summer day
After many ravenous crow attacks
on baby birds and the semblance of
peace and order returning upon hearing
the gentle cooing of a mourning dove.

And a cold winter afternoon…
long, long. ago…
inside a townhouse surrounded by piles of ice
and snow but always with cleared roads
and driveways by seven o'clock
An amaryllis and a bible on the coffee table
A place of healing refuge.
Two mourning doves on the snowy patio.

But no hyacinth saved by a dove.

Three budgies – one very mean
and two from Bowmanville
Hand fed named Lovekin and Tassil
And a death in my hand
just before leaving for Mexico.

(continued)

And talk of me having a gray heron
as a totem animal because I had seen many
and she had seen none.
Even herons catching voles and wacking them
on the ground until manageable.

Copying a robin picture when seven
seeing twenty-five in berry bushes in the snow;
coming to my front door
and having a robin fly in my face
realizing later that it had eaten all of the
holly berries off the female bush on the right.

The mynah birds in Hawaii
waiting as anxious as I
for the bananas, guava and mangoes
to ripen.

English sparrows on a stoop
creating more sparrows
with me watching intently
like a nasty voyeur.

The red-breasted grosbeaks
in my cherry tree and the
apple tree down the street
petals falling gently.

Outstretched wings of
a Red-Shouldered Hawk
revealing God's presence
and His promise

Pigeons on hospital roofs
with distinctly similar colouring
as if from the very same gene pool
creating their usual poopy mess.

But until now never a hyacinth
that was saved by a dove
For I believe that the dove
was saved by the hyacinth
And I am sticking to my story
on this cold winter morning
in the here and now.

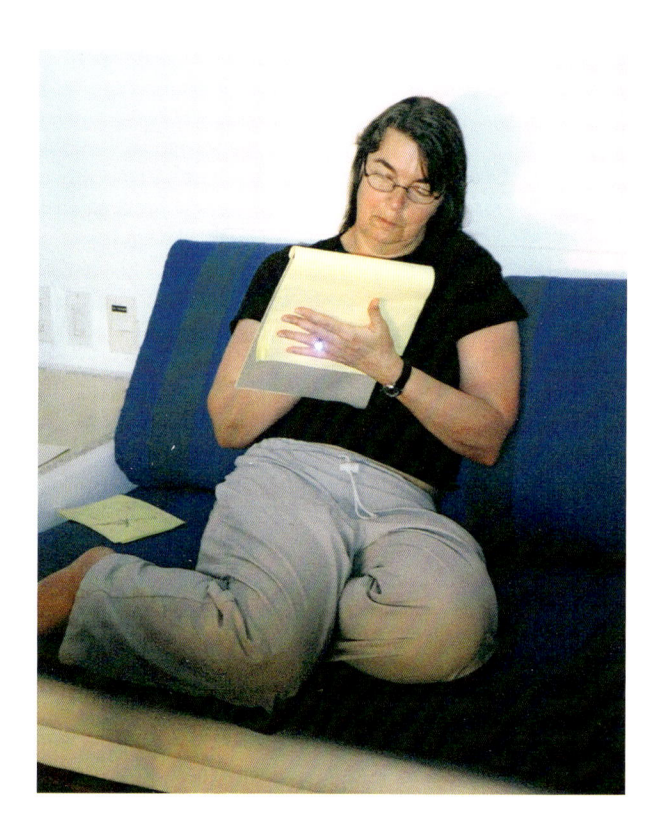

Cutting Roses on a Summer Morning

Cutting roses on a summer morning,
Straw, white, navy;
Stone cottage mansion garden
Faded, wilted and yet
The fragrance still touches your nostrils.
Are you as contented as you look
With tomato plants greening and roses blooming?
Ownership is apparent;
Cutting your roses on a summer morning

Glasses, white, gray;
Low-rise apartment house.
Bolding, magnificent view as
The colour and perfection reach you
Who are you?
What right do you have to nip the brevity of summer?
What right except of me cutting roses on a summer morning.

ON THE WANE

And after a night of crazy
But being very very careful
I am totally, inexorably
mentally and physically exhausted.
Even my spirit feels on the wane.
I resort to shortbread cookies
and dark chocolate-covered almonds,
And Words With Friends and red knee socks
To offset my *wane*

I try to cleanse ***My*** *"wane"* with green juice,
        But to no avail.

I visit a family member with pneumonia,
Watch the CN tower at midnight
Dance in gray striped knee socks
Buy a new game
And drink more green juice.

Re-pot my violets…

Hefty OneZip

I have an encounter involving a zipper –
An imaginary zipper under the chin
And running the full length of the neck.
"If I can just undo this zipper, I can get out of here"
Are the words uttered.

Death and rebirth by zipper
Why not?
What a concept
No wonder I have always admired zippers.

Such a unique invention
Even more mind-boggling than Velcro
And now elevated to a new level
Didn't a certain poet unzip his skin
and sit in his bones while writing?

Cicadas do it
After 17 years in the ground
they crawl out of the ground
onto the tallest tree trunk
and unzip

Butterflies
and dragonflies
and moths
do it too

Hummm

Watching Time Pass

Oh no, this year it will not be so splendid;
And yet the bees know differently.

The sky is barely visible
Through the white-tufted branches
And the black switches
Meander through the sunlit greens.

All time is planned to view the bloom
And I must stand still
To watch the blossoms pass.

Some petals drift to earth too soon
Since creatures of flight
Within the blossom centres find delight.

Too brief a passage
And yet too fine
To become tarnished by time.

Be still and know that I am God.
        Psalm 46:10

A Reason for Gardenphobia

The garden going on without us
Leaps brick borders
In a single bound,
Scales brick walls
And claws her way
Across the window screen.

The children hear her breathing
As they sleep,
And wake to find tendrils
Of deadly nightshade
Just beginning to twist
Around their necks.

The succulent red shiny berries
Beckon them without mercy
While a lingering odour
Provides a narcotic warning
Urging them to flee
And yet to dream on.

A tiny plastic hand
Exhumed from sandy soil
Speaks clearly of recent bygone days
And of pre-plastic times as well:

A century ago,
The Battle of Trowel
Was fought on this very site;
The rusted remains
Laid to rest
Under a rotting pine box.

Until today,
As we scratch
Through the dirt
With our bare hands,
Putting you, Fair Lady
Into plastic garbage bags,

Trying to pretend
The garden is no longer going on without us.

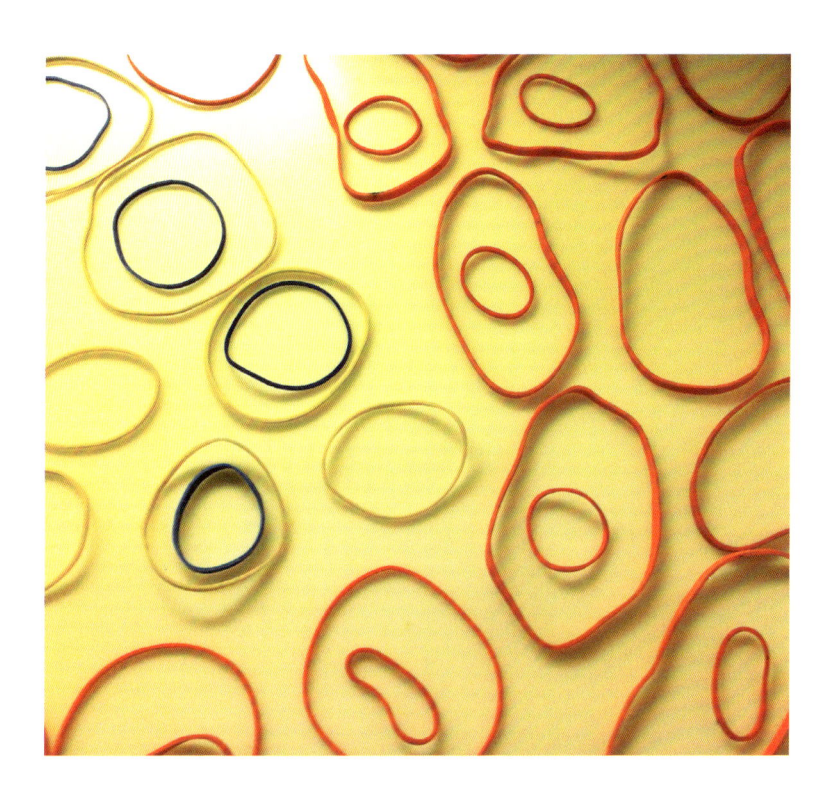

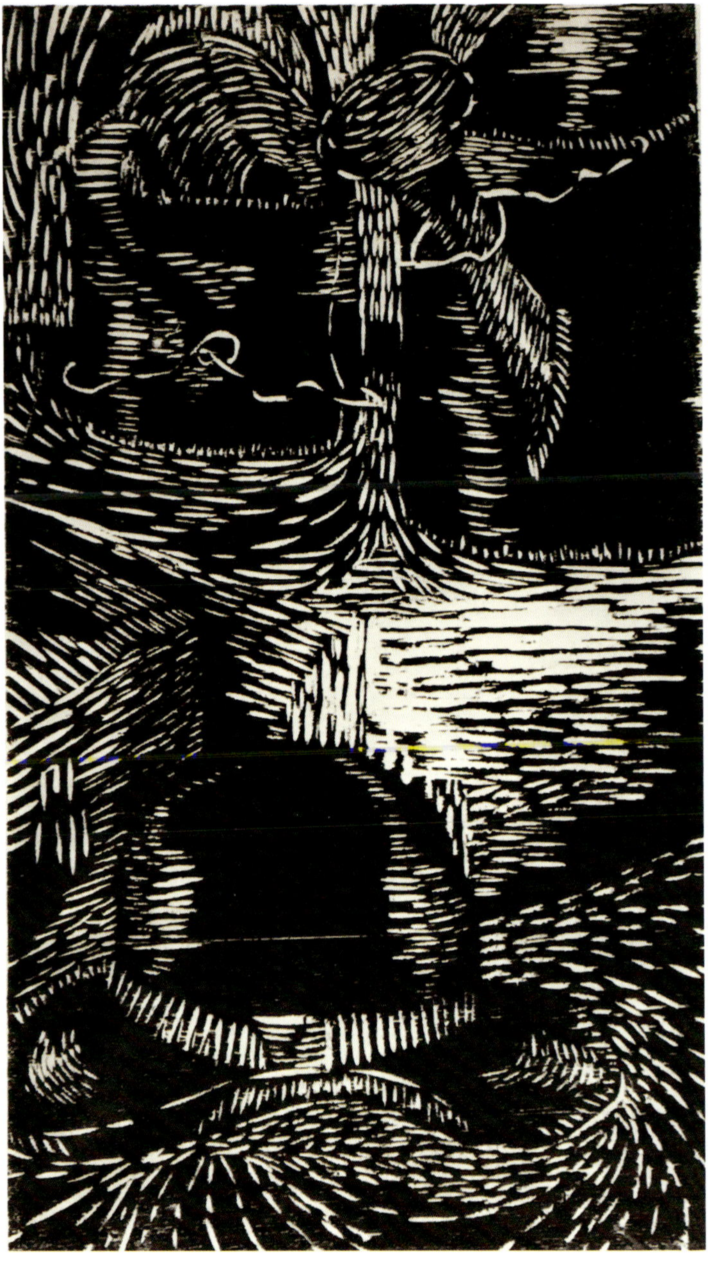

Odds and Ends

Diamonds and rubies and pearls
and a dozen long-stemmed roses,
three thousand pairs of shoes:
to some these are treasures.

A small stone glittering in the sun,
a handful of bird nest
and a crumpled ball of dandelions
on the counter:

In the lawn these are monsters
but in the hand,
glowing yellow hope.

These are His Gifts.

Once considered
they speak of
greater and lesser worth,
the dichotomy of very valuable junk,
precious garbage,
a dozen long-stemmed weeds.

In light of the re-assessment of value,
this life is simply a ceramic trinket box
full of important odds and ends
that must be kept safe from harm.

BLACK COFFEE

Making coffee also
but what do I know?

Every night I ask him:
Are you finished with your coffee?
He says yes.
In the dark of night
I pour the remaining coffee
around the base of our holly bushes
since they love acidic soil
and are thriving.

now – no milk... but could do almond

For Every Action

Yesterday I planted "calliope dark red" geraniums.
Dug the hole, amended the soil
with Mennonite compost mix
And in the process,
disturbed two holes
made by our resident chipmunk –
The one who always leaves footprints
in the first covering of snow
across our front doorstep.
From the evidence
our chipmunk had attempted
to dig his way back
into his nest:
He died digging.
Seems like it's impossible
for man or woman to co-exist
without consequences
Especially with the smaller of God's creatures –
Doesn't it?

Addendum:
'Calliope dark red' attracts butterflies, but kills chipmunks.

COTTAGE CONVERSATIONS

My parents built a retirement cottage on the shoreline of Weslemkoon Lake, Ontario in the 1970s. I added to that cottage over the years for my mother's enjoyment, and for the comfort of family and friends. I first took Janet and her daughter, Laura, there to meet my mother in September, 1999. That was the weekend I asked Janet for permission to kiss her, and she said yes. A magical moment we often recalled together, because it seemed like every loon on the lake was singing its haunting spiritual call to us at that moment... echoing across the water. In 2001 I designed a cottage and had it built for just us, next door to my mother's larger "family cottage." Some of the happiest, most carefree moments, days, weeks and months of our life together took place at Weslemkoon Lake. Warm days of golden light. Magnificent sunsets. Glorious fall color. Family times together roasting marshmallows in the fire pit. And cool fall evenings in our cozy cottage warmed by a wood burning fireplace. We played in babbling brooks flowing in the springtime, explored the forest around us in the summer and throughout the magnificent fall season into October – and experienced the absolute silence and beauty of winters walking together on the frozen lake.

94 *Sailing* – "You will not get wet," then we nearly drowned.

96 *No Cell Phone Access* – A 20-mile wilderness drive.

97 *Off to Paul and Mary's House* – A decade of memories.

98 *Playing Doctor* – We were a team from the beginning.

100 *Repairing Dragonfly Wings: Chapter 1* – Repairing a curtain.

101 *Repairing Dragonfly Wings: Chapter 2* – God's hand.

102 *The Year of the Mouse* – Mystery. Tension. Humor.

104 *Playing With Fire* – Cottage conversation turns to fire events.

105 *The Apple* – Marina owner recounts Janet's gallbladder attack.

106 *Water Damage* – From conflict to disconnect to isolated angst.

108 *Jonathan and Nicole:* – Newlyweds share.

109 *Happy Thanksgiving* – Noting the outside world's madness.

111 *Reminiscing about My Legacy* – Cemetery contemplations.

Sailing

And when he asked me if I wanted to go sailing
on that mild and sunny day in April
I couldn't resist and said "Yes but will I get wet?"
and he said "No"
but I still emptied my pockets of cash and Kleenex
and since I had never sailed before
he put me in charge of the tiller
and we headed out across West Bay in the late afternoon.

Without a chance to utter the word "suddenly"
a monumental gust of wind caught the sail
and we headed for the largest rock in sight.

Upon instruction and while trying to get out of the way,
I leapt for the main pole as the captain lunged for the tiller.

When we hit the rock, I remained firmly intact
but the captain was now in the icy water
with one shoe missing.

He climbed onto the rock and held fast to the boat
just long enough to tell me that I must exit
and in so doing, get wet,
which I did.

The sailboat then capsized.

A lone power boat zoomed by
but my cries for help
were drowned out by the engine noise.

Throwing his second shoe into the lake,
the captain then re-entered the water
and righted our vessel
but sailing homeward was impossible
and so we dismantled the sail and retrieved the paddles.

Seemingly forever, we dug in against the wind and current,
until the main pole crunched into an overhanging tree
at the far side of our docking bay and the captain
entered the icy water once more to disentangle us.

We thawed out in the hot tub
talking the while about family members
lost in icy waters
but we did not deliver an official gratitude prayer
since those were days of silent homage
however I am saying one now:

Praise for an Omnipotent God,
our Steadfast Captain,
Solid Rock
and Faithful Protector.

No Cell Phone Access

The second to last leg of the journey to the cottage is a long, dark and isolating road, especially when you are by yourself, on that road for the first time. My mission was to get to the end of it, but about three-quarters of the way along I wasn't quite sure if I was on the right road. Lately, I have had a tendency to miss turn-offs, and then have to backtrack to the correct off-exit. However, on a road that is quickly turning into the black of night, I did not want to have to go back. As I drove deeper into the woods while looking for a clearing, a sense of panic overtook me. For the first time on my journey, my hands began to sweat and I started to devise strategies for a "worst-case" scenario. What if I did have to turn back and couldn't find the exit point in the pitch darkness? I would be looking for a road that said "Weslemkoon Lake" and a small sign on the left. Both very easy to miss in the dark, and heading in the opposite direction. I started to take mental note of memorizing the locations of cottages and houses. A car came up behind me forcing me along the road, but I soon pulled over to let it pass. I wondered if I should have asked that lone driver for help, but felt too vulnerable to do so. As I neared the end of the road absolutely nothing was recognizable. Every rock and every tree were foreign to me. And then I came to a clearing and a sign. Yes, I had made the right decision to forge ahead. I saw a mosquito-bitten man waving at me, and a black dog who was wagging her tail. They had been anticipating my arrival for 45 minutes, and had imagined me in a number of compromising situations on the dark and isolating road. Safe again and in familiar surroundings, I was able to laugh about my fears and apprehensions, and marvel at the fact that I had reached my destination without having to retrace my steps.

OFF TO PAUL AND MARY'S HOUSE

And we are not wearing our brown galoshes
As we climb the wet and prickly hill
Along the hydro line behind the cottage
With a basket of Grey Goose and Johnny Walker Blue
Not yet knowing about fish fry and blueberry pie
Red and yellow mushrooms in early summer
Asparagus ends caught in the disposal
Nel's surprise visit to a dying B.J.
A near-death experience at the beaver dam
Hand-holding in prayer at a Thanksgiving feast
Christmas laughter in Tweed
A new house on a road with piles of firewood
A hidden fish-filled lake and greens from the garden
A scratch repair in the driveway
Not yet knowing about a red sedan and a funeral plan
And we are not wearing our brown galoshes
As we enter the valley of the shadow of death
With a basket of Love Joy and Peace and a Package of Figs
Knowing that we shall dwell in the house of the Lord forever

Playing Doctor

Doctor Foster enters
Dragging his patient
Across the porch floor.
(We all have our crosses to bear)

Need some help?
Asks Dr. Franklin.
The patient is given
A thorough examination
Prepped for surgery
Carried into the operating room.
(Two young interns observe from the gallery)

Dr. Foster proceeds:
Scrubs in,
Requires duct tape and scissors,
Dr. Franklin searches,
Remembers old adhesive tape
From last appendix operation.
(The one where son's life was threatened)

Hours pass:
Track repaired
Cord adjusted
Lysol sprayed
Hands touch,
Souls unite.
(Dr. Foster takes a Pepsi break)

Slats and valance re-installed:
Open-heart surgery is complete,
The operation is a success.
(The patient remains dead and blind)

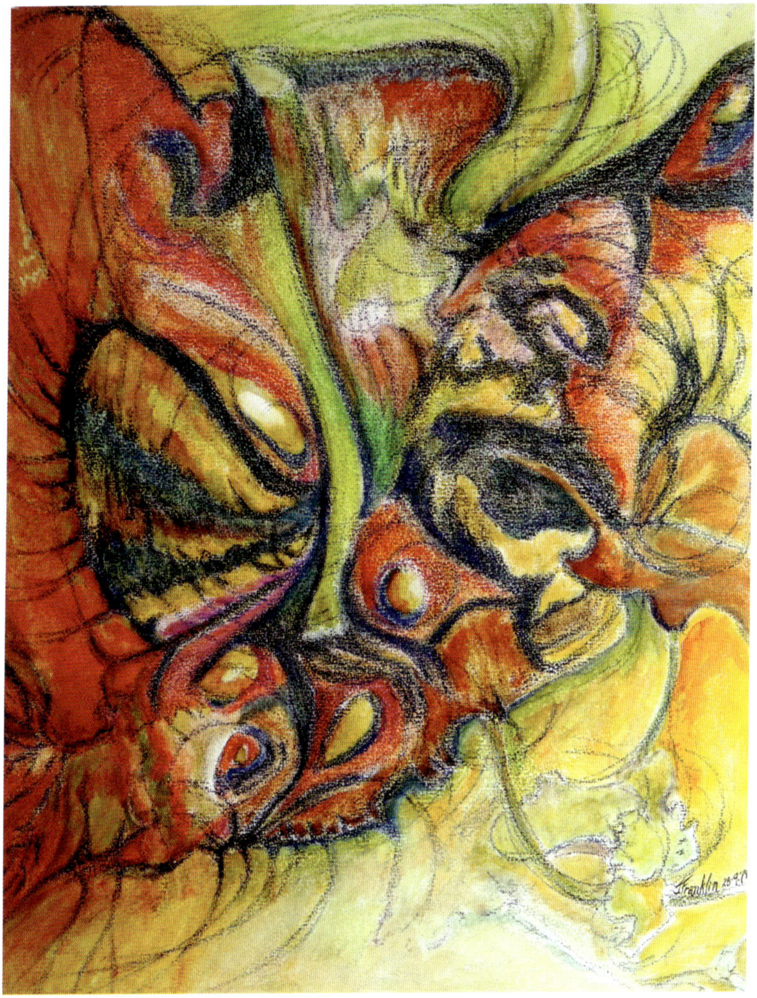

REPAIRING DRAGONFLY WINGS

Chapter 1

One day God said:
I want you to repair dragonfly wings

I said:
I don't have the time

One night God said:
I want you to repair dragonfly wings

I said:
I don't know how

One morning God said:
I want you to repair dragonfly wings

I said:
I don't have the proper thread

God continued to be patient with me

He kept me at the cottage for an eternity

Had me mend the hem of a new towel

Showed me a sewing box in need of sorting

And then He went on vacation

REPAIRING DRAGONFLY WINGS

Chapter 2

In the sewing box I found:

Large Golden-Eye
10 SHARPS 3/9
MADE IN JAPAN
Needles
Warranted 100 yards
PURE 'A' SILK
WATERTOWN CONN
Thread
(In the precise color
of dragonfly wings)

I immersed myself
In the Book of Ecclesiastes
And the Book of Psalms

One hundred years later God said:
I want you to repair dragonfly wings

I said:
Yes Lord, Thy will be done

And so it came to pass
Amen

THE YEAR OF THE MOUSE

I know we are in for trouble when I dropped a
HoneyNut Cheerio on the kitchen floor at the
cottage and a mouse scurried out to retrieve it
in broad daylight.

The battle lines had been drawn
and Richard went to Bancroft for ammunition.

Regular snap-traps loaded with peanut butter were
deemed too messy and would not last the winter,
and so, he settled for boxes of dry, gray mouse pellets
instead: a Warfarin compound that causes mice to
neatly and silently bleed to death internally.

As we exit our summer abode, ten or twelve packets
of mouse food lie open and available to any mouse
who reentered indoors for the next eight months.

Upon our return in late spring nothing appeared
to be out of order; the mounds of Warfarin had
disappeared as we had anticipated.

At nightfall, Richard who had trained himself
to fall asleep quickly prepared for bed in ten seconds,
and was fast asleep in another five (in the one bed that
we had left with sheets on it in October).

Alone and in the heavy silence of the night, I decided to probe a tad deeper regarding the "goings-on" in our absence. I ventured into Mother's room and turned back the duvet. A "contained" pile of Warfarin was amassed next to the lower pillow edge. Next I checked in the living room. Under every imaginable cushion, more Warfarin surfaced. Between the towels and face clothes in the bathroom – more Warfarin.

The table had turned in my evening solitude, weakness, I was beginning to feel very vulnerable. Having seen a dog poisoned by the very same Warfarin compound and having witnessed the results of uncontrollable bruising and weeping of the skin, my mind was unsettled to say the least.

Spiraling downward into paranoia, I know my only recourse was sleep. I turn on the bedroom light and cautiously draw back the duvet cover next to my now sleeping husband. Two Warfarin pellets neatly and discretely placed on my side of the bed appeared. No doubt from a certain mouse's perspective "revenge was as sweet as a HoneyNut Cheerio".

I removed the pellets, covered the area with a towel, and prayed to God for Warfarin protection.

A single mouse had me on the run.

PLAYING WITH FIRE

We learn that a neighbor
Across the bay
Saw smoke
And came to investigate

Someone had built a fire
During our season of drought
Igniting the roots of our trees
Like giant candle wicks
That burned underground
Toward our cottage.

Upon further investigation
We find a birchbark-covered lean-to
With a stone-ringed "surface" fire pit
Under tall evergreen trees
In the tinderbox thicket of the forest
And firewood stacked neatly
In preparation for the next burn.

We are reminded of a woodstove pipe
Installed without insulation, through
A wooden roofed cottage next door
And neighbors who long ago rallied
To subdue the inferno.

A recent conversation
With our State Farm Agent
Confirming a million-dollar policy
Does nothing to console us.

The Apple

I lie writhing on the back seat of the car,
Friends and family watching over me,
Some praying and some wondering what to do.

Sensing their concern,
I look up reassuringly and say:
"It's okay I just ate an apple."

Eve stands before the Lord,
Yesterday's paradise lost
Her husband's trust betrayed,
She wonders if she will ever find forgiveness.

Dropping her eyes
And hiding her nakedness
She says through her tears:
"But I only ate an apple."

A loving God looks down on the world
Knowing His Son has overruled the law
And not only forgives Eve
But heals our every sickness.

Fear and worry are replaced by grace,
And God now says:
"Go ahead enjoy the fruit."

Janet wrote this poem in collaboration with her friend Ruth Blanchard.

WATER DAMAGE

Eight o'clock
We shake hands
No crokinole, shuffle board or Chinese checkers tonight.

I brush my teeth
And then decide to wash my feet
In the fancy sink
Without an overflow drain.

The tap is running
The plug in-place
As I return to my room
To go under cover and decompress with my castor-oil pack
But my feet are srill covered with
bits from the woods

I open my door
And notice a gentle glistening stream
Running down the hallway
Towards the cupped oak flooring
Already damaged when the dishwasher
Was installed incorrectly

I say "oh ____" and
Grab all available toweling
To swab the deck
As I swiftly disengage the drain plug

I hear snoring across the hallway
And determine to deal with this soggy scenario
With God's assistance alone

An hour passes swiftly
And then two
As towels are put out to dry overnight
On the porch. Then retrieved ten minutes later
And folded neatly on a rubberized sheet
On the floor of my room.
A pair of water-soaked moccasins remain
I turn them upside down to maximize air exposure.
Back under my duvet,
My heart is pounding
As I deep-breathe to decompress.
I get up and check the sink
Before lights out.

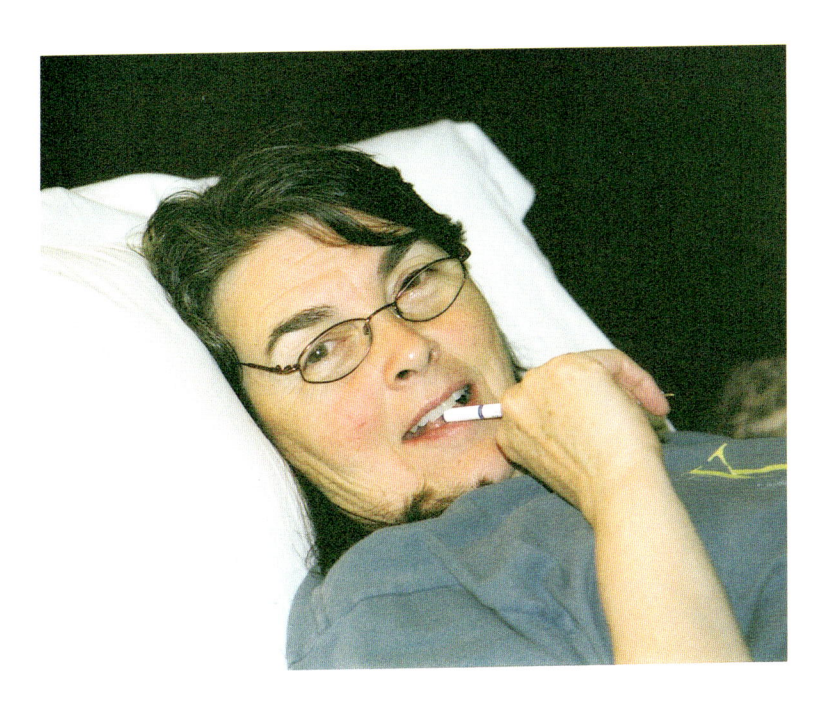

JONATHAN AND NICOLE:
A HUMMINGBIRD MOMENT

I hope some day to be able to share with you a drawing
that is very significant to me: Words will not do it justice,
but let me try.

*The picture is comprised of a hummingbird directly in the face
of a raven, suspended in flight… a hummingbird's breath away from
each other.*

I have never '"liked" crows
But feel that they have probably gotten a "bad rap",
just like sharks and wolves.
But hummingbirds,
even though they can be aggressive,
are like rainbows,
elusive and ethereal.
Whenever I think of a hummingbird,
I am comforted.
And so, I am so very glad
that a hummingbird touched down on you and Jonathan
as you lay together in our hammock
at Weslemkoon Lake this summer.
And that you shared the moment with us all
with a sense of awe and excitement.

May your lives be filled with hummingbird moments,
as you bravely jump off of cliffs together,
and venture amidst flocks of ravens.

Happy Thanksgiving

As the world goes mad
With the beheadings of Christian children
And a suicide with slit wrists and a leather belt,
We are blessed with shuffleboard tournaments,
Campfires, group swims across the bay,
And fresh corn from the roadside stand
South of Madoc.
Chinese checkers and apple pie.
Children recently back from camp.
A warm bed after a cold dark night
Almost lost on the lake between rock
And harbour
But plenty of prayer and gratitude
For the potential of an every day "Happy Thanksgiving".

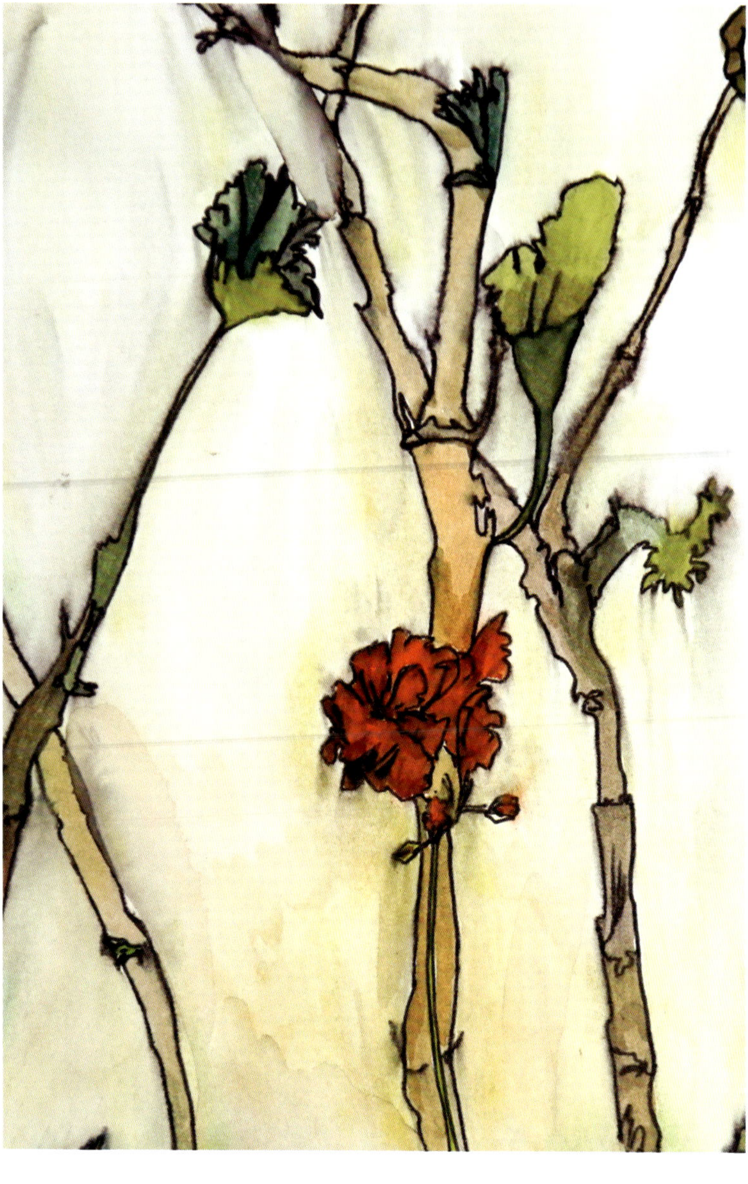

Reminiscing About My legacy

Contemplating death while reburying the rotted corncobs and black banana peels (reminiscent of the OJ Simpson trial)
I have come to a conclusion regarding my perfect demise:
I am at the cottage working in my compost pile unearthing avocado pits (reminiscent of my daughter)
when I have a sudden heart attack and die almost instantly while face-planting in some old corn husks (reminiscent of the kind used as bandages in the American Civil War)
I have found my resting place and so no need to call 911 for helicopter backup.
When you find my dead body, you may hold me in your arms while God's army of Angels comes to guide my soul to its resting place where I shall see His Face (reminiscent of Moses on the mountain top receiving the Ten Commandments)
No worries,
My death shall not be as shocking as my broken arm while roller skating.

Molokai Conversations

Molokai is 40 miles long and five miles wide. A simple, no frills, quiet place. The last bastion of old Hawaii with magnificent views, pristine quiet beaches, and a family-based community filled with aloha spirit. A commercial pilot once told me that he was always spiritually moved whenever he flew over Molokai. From 20,000 feet he saw an aura presence around the entire island like no other island on earth in his experience. When I first stepped foot on the island in 1976 it instantly felt like home. I purchased land there in 1986 but had given up the idea of building on my property…until I went there with Janet in March of 2000, and Molokai instantly felt like home to her as well. We both felt a heightened God presence. We vacationed there annually until our home was under construction in 2005, and then extended our time to more than five months each winter, until Janet's 2010 breast cancer operations. Janet and I were married on March 9, 2003 in Grace Episcopal Church on Molokai. Our marriage was a spontaneous idea of Janet's. One morning over breakfast she said, "Let's get married on Molokai next Saturday" – giving me one week to make it a fabulous moment in our lives. And it was.

114 *I Could Sing of Your Love Forever* – Our love song.

117 *Wind. Rain. Sun. Moon. Waves. Ocean* – Journal entry. Joy.

119 *The Day the World Went Wild* – Wind madness.

120 *Chasing the White Rabbit* – Evening drive home from church.

122 *The Snails Have Me on the Run* – Wonderful storytelling.

123 *Divine Succulent* – Haiku.

124 *Hele Pohaku* – Hawaiian "moving" rock spirits connection.

125 *My Hibiscus was Yesterday* – Joy of our magical citrus grove.

126 *Cow Manure* – Manure order for the cherry tomato garden.

127 *At the Co-op* – Continues the Cow Manure conversation.

128 *A Rainbow Vision* – A journal entry. Spiritual life on Molokai.

129 *Banana Day* – A journal entry. Our first banana harvest.

130 *All About Bob* – A very "Janet" story about a garden insect.

132 *Our Anniversary Team-Building Exercise* – *God Moment.*

I Could Sing of Your Love Forever
(© Martin Smith/Delirious? 1994)

Over the mountains and the sea
Your river runs with love for me
And I will open up my heart
And let the healer set me free

I'm happy to be in the truth
And I will daily lift my hands

For I will always sing of when your
love came down.

I could sing of your love forever
I could sing of your love forever
I could sing of your love forever
I could sing of your love forever
I could sing of your love forever
I could sing of your love forever
I could sing of your love forever

Oh I feel like dancing
It's foolishness I know
But when the world has seen the light
They will dance for joy
Like we are dancing now

I could sing of your love forever
I could sing of your love forever
I could sing of your love forever
I could sing of your love forever
I could sing of your love forever
I could sing of your love forever
I could sing of your love forever

Note: This song was being played by Scotty Schafer the first time Janet and I walked into Grace Episcopal Church on Molokai for Sunday service in March of 2000. It became our song… touched our hearts profoundly. It was our God song… and our soulmate love song. And over the years 2001-2009 the playing of *I could sing of your love forever* seemed to always being played by Scotty as we approached the church entrance, to everyone's surprise. There are no coincidences. And, of course this was one of the songs played during our wedding ceremony there on March 9, 2003.

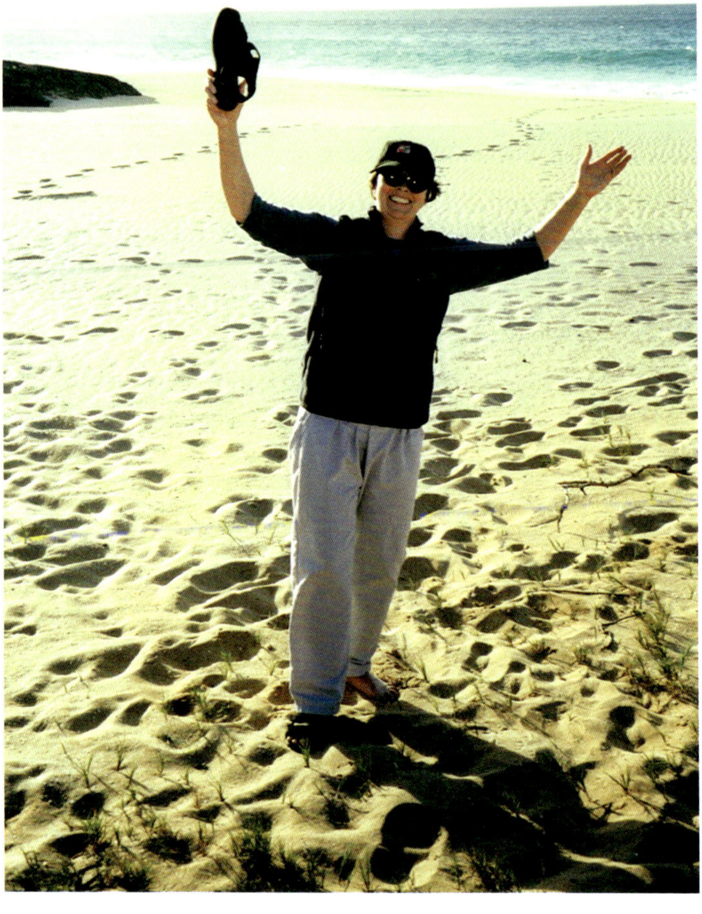

WIND. RAIN. SUN. MOON. WAVES. OCEAN

wind	Haven't got a care in the world
rain	Thoughts on my mind
sun	wheels on the road
moon	(road on your wheels)
waves	my mind on Your thoughts
ocean	mist on the mountain
	(Mountain on Your mist)

      Your voice in my ears
      My ears in Your voice
A smile on my face
A face on Your smile
    mud on my shoe
wind in my hair
    sun in my eyes
(bugs in my teeth)
And a whole lot of love in my heart

Before the rain
thoughts on my mind
My mind on Your thoughts

Before the rain   **After the rain**

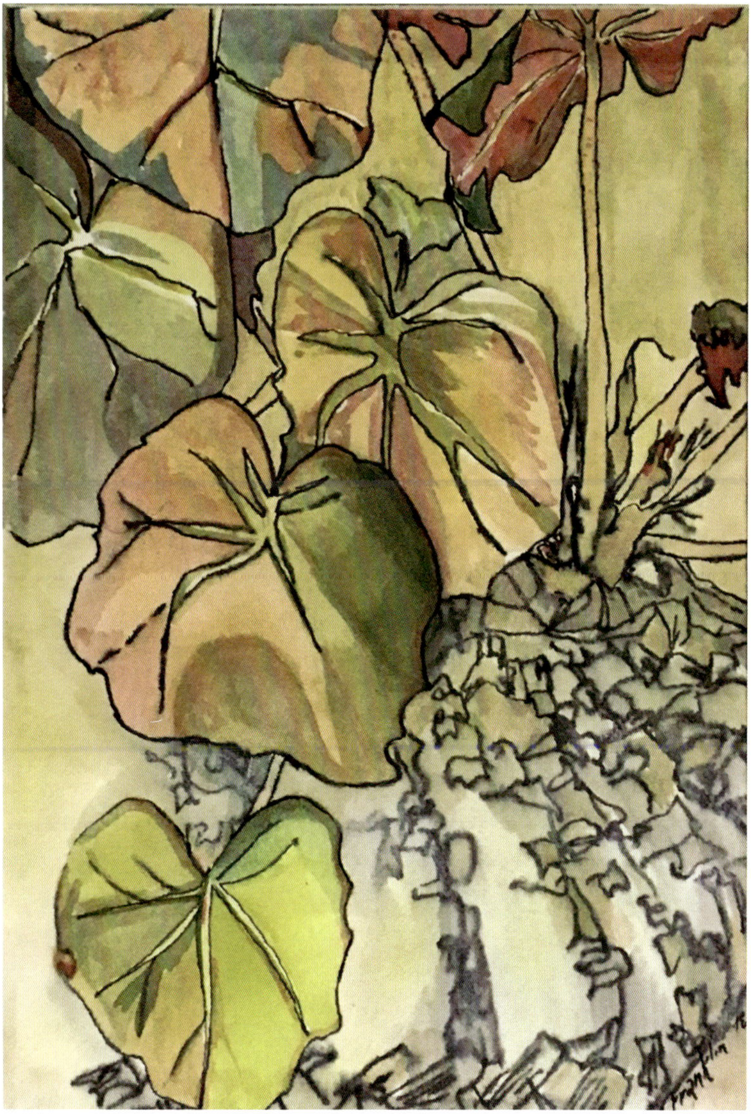

THE DAY THE WORLD WENT WILD

Pink sky in the morning
Everyone take warning.

The wind has a way of getting everyone a little bit crazy. Especially when it shreds the weigela, and whips all of the covers off the lanai furniture. That's the time for serious action, like weaving your pick-up truck around the obstacle course of newly planted Norfolk Pine, and erecting walls (at least three of them) out of cinder block. Walls that make the wind even angrier and cause it to blow even harder. So hard in fact that a pod of whales breached right over the wall and landed on the anthurium, peace lily and areca palm trees. Their tails even whipped the corner of the house dislodging and breaking several slate tiles. Time for action. Prayer was a necessity. Acknowledging that God knows how to keep the stars in the sky and the sun on the rise, we knelt and apologized for trying to tame the wind. We asked God to reverse time and return us to pre-wall days. And then we waited and listened. "Take down the walls" whispered the voice of many waters. And the command echoed throughout the dusty dry land, three times.

We removed the walls, the overly-sensitive plants, and a courageous dolphin led the whales out to the sea. The wind ceased its howling, and settled into a gentle breeze. God's paradise had been restored.

CHASING THE WHITE RABBIT

At the corner of Kalua Koi Road
And Pa Loa Loop
We encounter the white rabbit

Beneath the blackest sky
Between side thickets of haole koa
Along the blackest pavement

A large white rabbit
Lop lop lopping
Caught in the beam of our headlights

In the car
Out of the car
The hunt is on

No bait (except two squares of sweet potato pie)
No trap (not even a cardboard box)
No ammunition (except for our limited rabbit knowledge)

And our imaginations:
"I don't want to find him dead on the road in the morning"
                    "Are you trying to catch him?"
"He may have a heart attack if we follow him too far or too fast"
                    "Watch out for scratching and biting"

"Let's chase him all the way home"

In the car
Out of the car
The hunt continues

He veers off the road to rest
With his back legs extended
And his belly nestled against the ground

And then cuts across the road
But is suddenly swallowed up
By The Cat Lady's driveway

Leaving us with only the most vivid memory
Of the whitest rabbit on the darkest road
On a magical Molokai night

The Snails Have Me On The Run

Last year when I was cleaning out a roach and flea-infested apartment, I was given a succulent that snails love. Not just any snails, but the Giant African Snail on the International Wanted Dead Not Alive List.

This particular snail cuts perfectly round holes in perfectly formed leaves without an inkling of guilt or remorse. Unlike the Chinese Rose Beetle which turns all leaves to a lacy disaster area, this snail is more discreet and appears to abandon its food after taking one large bite. (Recently, I observed this same behaviour in my two-year-old-grandson who used the same approach with a plate of crackers.) Also, according to internet information, this particular snail is disease-ridden and prolific.

All of this bad news saddens me since these snails have amazing shells, are highly adaptable, and do not sting like centipedes or scorpions. They do not fly into my hair like giant cockroaches are prone to do, or eat my ceiling like certain brown ants that I have come to know only too well.

Unlike geckos who run when they see me coming and then poop on me from a higher vantage point, Giant African Snails just sit there when exposed, waiting for me to throw them over the barbwire fence as far as my undeveloped pitching arm will allow.

My husband has alerted me that they can and will find their way back to their favourite food and water but I usually try not to listen. On one particular day, however, I decided to change my snail control strategy.

Wearing my faux-leather construction/gardening gloves, I removed yet another Giant African Snail from beneath my favourite succulent and placed it under the largest rock that I could lift. I justified my destructive behaviour by mentally noting that I was now composting. I did not raise the rock to survey the damage.

When I returned a week later, I rolled the rock away. I found nothing. I tried a second and third rock. Still I found no evidence that the snail ever existed but next to the edge of the ficus groundcover, I saw a much smaller version of my original snail and placed it in the middle of the walkway and observed its slimy journey towards my treasured succulent.

I returned a couple of hours later to find that the snail had retreated into its shell and seemed as light as air. In fact, light enough to blow away in the incessant wind when my attention moved elsewhere.

The day before leaving Molokai, I checked underneath my prized succulent and the smaller snail was there. I picked it up and tossed it over the barbwire fence.

By my estimation, it should take much longer for the smaller snail to return. In fact, it shouldn't be back in business until the day before I set foot on Molokai once more.

Divine Succulent:

:a

::snail

:::has

::::me

:::::on

::::::the

:::::::run

Perfect Destruction

HELE POHAKU

Long ago and one by one
From the north shore to the south

The rocks were on the move
The rocks were on the move

Fish ponds, altars, terraces
Took many refugees in
Turning the rocks to "locals"

But the sea and silt followed
Armies with bulldozers came

The rocks began to move
The rocks began to move

From six-mile and the overpass
To the Papohaku shore
For Pele's fiery rage

The rocks are on the move
The rocks are on the move

Still today and one by one
From the east shore to the west

To Richard the Rockmason
With much love--
Janet
March 8, 2007 Molokai Hawaii

My Hibiscus Was Yesterday

Two days ago
I ventured to the grove
Where a double pink hibiscus
Was about to bloom.

Upon my return
My hibiscus was yesterday
But my today was filled with miracles:

Fresh green growth
Atop the breadfruit
Bearing two sandpaper sheathes
For polishing kukui nuts.

Inch-long papayas
And fruit-producing white flowers
On the beach napaka and lime tree.

A pot-bound plumeria
Begging to be planted
Near to where it stood
And volunteer ferns
Nestled in rock wall crevices.

A large bunch of bananas
On the verge of ripening
Needing to be picked
And stored in the barn
Before the banana birds' arrival.

And as always
God everywhere
But especially in His oasis
In this desert place.

Cow Manure

Ring! Ring! Ring!

Hello I say

Hello, she says, who is this?
I am Janet, who are you?

I am Kelsey from Hikiola Co-op
Is someone there named "Richard Foster"?

Yes he's my husband
He's not here right now
Can I take a message for him?

His cow manure has come in
Can he call me?

Oh the cow manure…
It's actually *my* cow manure
Richard always gives me cow manure
For my birthday and Valentine's Day

There are 15 bags, she says

Oh, I say, they must be for Christmas as well
Thank you so much, I'm very excited

I'll put the bags aside, she says

Thank you, thank you, thank you, I say.

At The Co-Op

Hi I'm Richard Foster
I'm here for the cow manure
I understand that you talked with my wife Janet.

Yes, oh yes, she told me that you give her sh**
For her birthday and Valentine's Day

Yes I do, I say.
And she gives me twice as much back.

"Ah yes," says the man standing behind me, "that's how it works."

Note: *None of the names of those who were guilty of partaking in this exchange has been altered and I would like to know the name of the man who was standing behind Richard.*

A Rainbow Vision

And I see God's hand outstretched
To touch Adam's outstretched finger
On the Sistine Chapel ceiling
Transforming Adam's hand into a rainbow.
Night falls, covering the rainbow
With blackness, the absence of all color
But the Word of God is inscribed
Breaking up the darkness from the inside out
And returning the rainbow to more than its former Glory
A Glory that was then partially hidden from the human eye
But existed in its entirety nonetheless
From the beginning of time.

BANANA DAY
May 22, 2008… Our First Harvest

-- ▸ grove to cut our 1st bunch
of bananas.
-- → Cut down "tree" also
-- → Sap sticky & stainy
up hill-- muddy/slippery
shoes caked in red dirt
+ soaked from playing with water
from hose in grove.
-- → dangerous – toss knife-saw
ahead of me in case I fall.
I think: "Here comes a sprained
ankle", as right foot twists
out of shoe.
-- → remove shoes
-- → path rocky & narrow –
I ask for God's help
path opens at top & levels out
-- → home: I sit to read
the Psalm of the day.

Psalm 18:
33   "He makes my feet like the feet of a deer,
          He enables me to stand on the heights"…
36   "You broaden the path beneath me
          so that my ankles do not turn"

All About Bob

Examining Desert Rose plant – *very* **eaten** – think, deer must be around still.
Then I see turquoise blue dot. What is it … part of a very large green caterpillar?

I try to identify him online, and read about a mother's story about her daughter's caterpillar and how they went to discoverlife.com, so I go there to zero in on what type of caterpillar this could be.
Color: green
Tail: yes
Eyes: Yes   *Hawkmoth:* An extensive list …
          Finally, **OLEANDER HAWKMOTH** … for sure!

I name my caterpillar "Bob" and put him in an old butter tub with plastic wrap loosely on top. He's looking a little lethargic. I try to energize him by opening the wrap just a tad.

Then I go to Maunaloa town to get meatballs and milk.

Three hours pass. I'm making dinner and Richard looks in Bob's container and says: *"Bob isn't in here."* I say: *"He has to be."* Richard says: *"He isn't."* I checked. *"You're right,* I say, *"he isn't."*

We check everywhere, high and low, over and under. NO BOB.

I waken @ 2:38 a.m. turn on the light so as not to step on BOB. Check high and low again for him. No go.

Days later Bob is still missing, but Bob #2, #3 and #4 show up crawling towards our house (to find Bob #1?). They head onto my Desert Rose plant. I put all three in an ice cream container… they eat and then look dead.

Pupating or what?

Our Anniversary Team-Building Exercise March 9th 2009

"Let's go to the beach and fly this kite to celebrate our anniversary," I said. You agreed and we headed down towards the beach.

Someone was sitting in a pick-up truck watching John and his nephews install the beams in the big house.

We "talked story" for about ten minutes or so and then we told our visitor that it was our anniversary and we were off to fly a kite together. "And if it's too windy to fly, we will try again tomorrow morning," I said, "because that's what marriage is all about – trying again and again – going back for more no matter what."

"Follow me," you said, as we crossed the dune.

We managed to get the kite in the air almost immediately but it soon crashed into a large kiave tree where it appeared to be stuck solid.

No problem. You borrowed the chainsaw from John's nephew and removed the offending section of the tree.

I reeled in the released length of string and reattached the hook onto the kite. We were off again and soaring high until the kite nose-dived into the lake that had been created on the beach by recent wave activity.

Our kite sank like a stone but you dragged it out and without hesitation held the water-logged kite up to catch the wind and it seemed to be flying better than ever.

Suddenly I realized that we were not alone. I felt the presence of the Third Party involved in our marriage and knew that with His help, our kite could soar into the stratosphere.

God told me that if I stayed focused and centered on Him, our kite would remain in the sky indefinitely.

I released all of the string on the reel and the kite soared non-stop for more than an hour.

As evening came upon us, I prayed for a civilized landing and we took turns reeling in and reeling in and reeling in, as the kite flew better and better until just before dark when it finally settled gently in the middle of Papohaku Beach.

"That was the best kite flying I have even seen," you said, and I replied, "God thanks you for the compliment."

What a Team!

FAMILY CONVERSATIONS

Janet was born in Toronto, Ontario, on January 10, 1949, and at the age of fourteen fell in love with Tom Franklin. They married in 1971 and birthed two children, Adam and Laura, seven years apart. Tom died suddenly of a massive heart attack in 1995. Janet's mother died of cancer when she was eighteen, and her father three years later, which resulted in a deep mother-daughter relationship with Tom's mother, Mary, that lasted until Mary's death at age 96, in 2015. In the summer of 1998 I introduced Janet to my mother, Dorcas, and they formed an immediate and deep connection. My mother died in 2014 at age 100. Many of the pieces in this chapter are about these mothers in Janet's life, but also about loving, fearful, humorous moments and conversations expressed as a mother herself. I've included a few pieces that date before my time that Janet shared with me over our years together – no doubt so that I could understand about some past experiences that shaped her. I believe Janet would approve of my including them in this first book of her writings.

136 *Family* – Deeper into what others call happenstance.

138 *Now You are Six* – Releasing son Adam to another's hands.

140 *The Saddest Moment that Won't Ever Happen* – Fear moment.

142 *Syllabication and Consternation* – On writing a sonnet.

145 *A Kiss* – With mother Mary in hospital – after hip surgery.

146 *Famous Last Words* – On confliction and pain as a teenager.

149 *Gran Tells the Story* – A grandma (mother Mary) incident.

150 *March 19, 2010* – Text conversation with daughter Laura.

152 *Did you know…This is the day Mom died* – On death/loss.

154 *First Meeting* – A poem for my Mom's 100th birthday.

156 *Watching* – Honoring granddaughter Leah's YouTube video.

158 *Without You* – Honoring my mother at her 90th birthday.

160 *Vitamin Time* – On Mom's pain management.

162 *I'm Still a Woman* – Mom faces a day in long-term care.

164 *The Well-Worn Path* – Cherishing mother Mary's giving heart.

166 *A Time* – Read at my mother's memorial, 2014.

168 *From Interment to Internment* – To an in-law's Japanese father.

170 *A Lesson Worth Learning* – If ego displaces love.

172 *We Are All On The Move* – Sisters sell their Toronto homes.

FAMILY

I was born into a Toronto, Ontario Canada family
Overlooking a cemetery.

My next family is USA born,
Aligned with Ohio, Pennsylvania, Massachusetts, New York,
Connecticut, New Hampshire and Maine.
We spend time on the farm at Burnt Cabins, PA
With the Family matriarch.
My husband died when I was forty-six
Leaving me with a fifteen and a seven-year-old to raise.

Three years passed and a new family evolved
One aligned with Dunnville, Kentucky, Connecticut, Ohio,
Florida and even Hawaii.
Another cross-border family with yet another mother.

And having lost a mother at age eighteen
I gained two more along the way
Two loving mothers who are living on into their nineties
With three hip replacements and two broken hips in total
And minds that can drift on foggy days
(But are sharp as a tack – when the sun shines)

A funeral takes us back to Dunnville
To honour a ninety-five-year-old sister and aunt
First and present family sit at opposite ends of the hall,
I do not take my seat with tea, sandwiches and cookies
But align with the son of my sister
And talk internet, hunting and fishing.

We do not go to the cemetery, but rather to a Lake Erie house
Where we align with yet another family group
Who live next to a ccmetery.
Returning under a full moon, on a very traveled road
To our Toronto house across the road from my original cemetery.

Now You Are Six

On the eve of your new beginning,
Something inside of me is dying:
I hear it groaning deep down in my gut.

At least when you're worried
You can still sleep.

You said that you would go
When you were six,
And being a child of your word,
So you shall.

New beginnings are always difficult:
Letting go is never easy,
Now we *both* know these truths.

I still feel that man creates
Many of his own problems;
Independence and competition
Are grossly overrated;
Emotional attachments
Are not given enough consideration.

When you are asleep,
I can still hold you closely,
But carrying you is almost impossible;
Your eight pounds
Ten and a half ounces
Have multiplied dramatically.

You've grown almost three inches
This past year,
Your Ronald McDonald growth chart
Says so.

Let's get into gear fairly easily
By remembering
That all situations
Have positive and negative sides.

We both shall grow
By facing all of what life has to offer
And by finding solutions
Both alone and together.

Believe me, at this point,
I also could say a swear word or two,
But carrying on,
Allow me to state my case:

Love is the sword
With which we have armed you,
Offer it wisely
And we both shall continue
To discover life's potential

The Saddest Moment that Won't Ever Happen

I know two mothers who have lost a son
And gained a daughter,
But I am not willing to be such a mother
And so, when my children are on the move
driving or flying, I worry
especially on blustery winter days with freezing
rain, black ice, plane wings that can't be de-iced,
and fifty-mile-per-hour wind gusts.
And so, when you text me to tell me that bad weather
cancelled your flight at 7:25 a.m. but that
you are taking off in fifteen minutes,
I worry.

Our last texted communication looks like

:)

Love you :)

Love you!

I am not worried but when the phone rings
I think the absolute worst, and am relieved
when I hear two snippets of very good news.

141

Syllabication and Consternation

Hello to words that knock upon my door,
Synapses mingle and rhyme bursts forth anew;
Syllabication doth complicate more,
Consternation, aggravation, ensue.

Rhythm seems forsaken as twisted rhyme turns
Sense to nonsense and content runs amok;
My fettered heart for a storyline yearns,
All to no avail and with no such luck.

And so lines pass and naught becomes a theme;
In the world of sonnets, form reigns supreme.

When Laura was asked to write a sonnet for her Grade 12 Writers' Craft Class, I, of course, became involved. Being accustomed to composing in a free-verse format, I found the restrictions of iambic pentameter: 4-4-4-2, A-B-A-B, C-D-C-D, E-F-E-F, G-G (rhyming couplet) to be almost overwhelming; however, I did manage to persevere and am still marveling that any meaningful poetry was ever written in such a disciplined and confining form.

Oops, I just realized that I am missing verse C-D-C-D. This omission could set me back by a few hours. Well, I should have known that the editing of "all rhyme and no reason" would not go smoothly.

It is now the morning-after-the-night-before of some stiff editing. I have spoken to Richard in Hawaii twice and Laura in Brantford once, eaten dinner and breakfast, and slept for eight broken hours waiting for Laura to arrive home safely. I am now ready to finish this sonnet. Here goes:

> This verse gone missing doth irk to the core,
> Process be damned, I seek an end in sight;
> Tasks yet unfinished, make my psyche sore
> As Molokai Man calls at evening light.
>
>   Amen

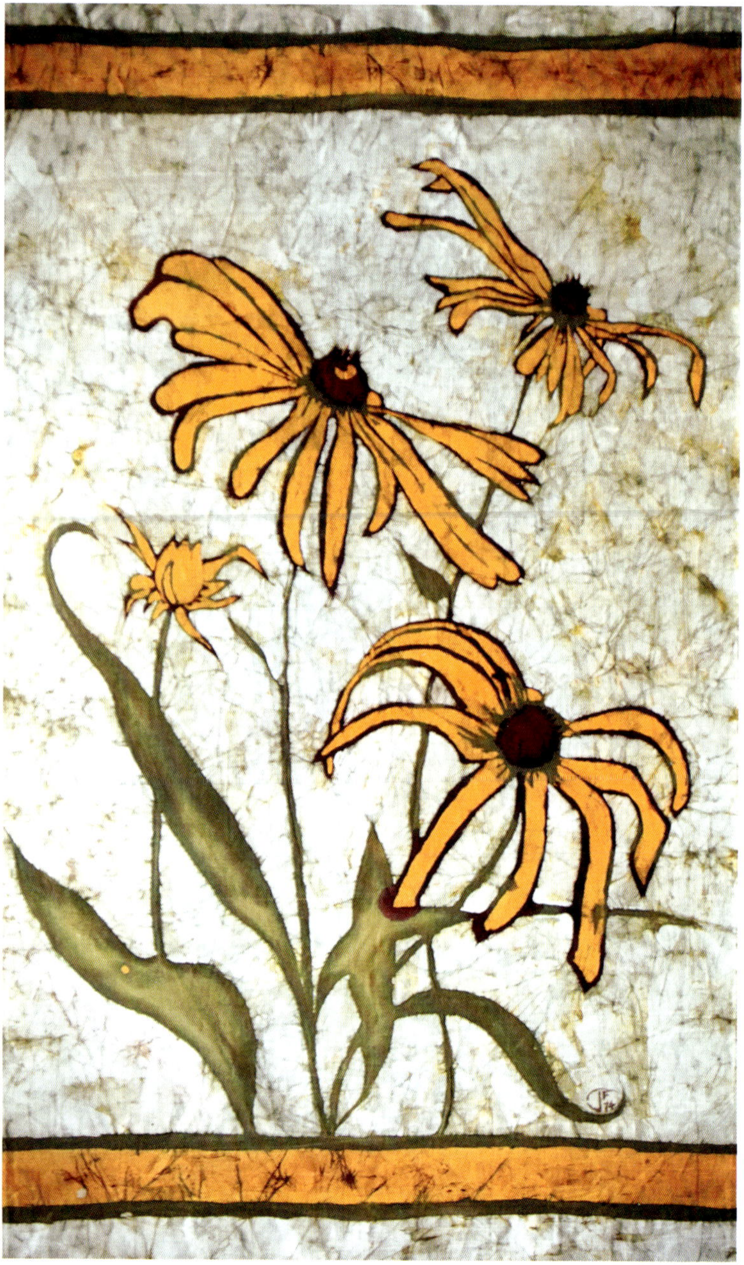

A Kiss

As we are returning
from that sunny place
down the hallway,

I am walking
and you are strapped
into your wheelchair
but propelling yourself
with your own legs and feet.

We meet another wheelchair occupant
who says:

you have a birthday coming up
and I know what your daughter
is going to give you---
a kiss---right here---
as she points to her cheek---
a big kiss and that's important
because it's a gift from the heart.

And I say: yes, you're right
and then we move on
while you say: she's cute.

As cute as you are, I say,
knowing our mutual dislike
for that word.

Famous Last Words

I was a teenager bursting forth
Taking on life with gusto
While your body and mind
Were closing down.

I wanted to go
off to the farm,
Stay out late
And not be accountable.

You wanted the opposite.

"I hope you know what you're doing,"
You said.
"I do," I said without hesitation.

You showed me a hole in your side
That wasn't healing
And I lied and hastily said:
"Don't worry, it'll be all right."
And then I went off to the farm
For the weekend.

You were sick
And I took over
some of your duties
But the spinach
was too expensive,
The milk was boiled
instead of heated,
And a "handful" of rice
in the soup,
Made the soup disappear.

You went to the hospital
and I wrote to you
about watering the houseplants
And you wrote back
about dreams of farmers' fields
and fresh green lettuce.

When I went to see you,
Your nails were yellow and brittle,
Your eyebrows were dishevelled,
And shockingly your mouth
Uttered only swear words.

Against my will, I started to cry.
You motioned to me as if to say:
"It's all right"

But I never went to the hospital again.

(continued)

I saw my father crying
In his dark basement room
And later I walked and wept
With my sister
In the park.

I always stayed out late.

And then one Saturday morning
The news of your death arrived
And for a brief second, the shock
Felt like relief:

And I was glad that you were gone.

Gran Tells the Story

Gran tells the story...

>about falling
>and hitting her head
>on ceramic tiles
>and spraining her right ankle
>to the point of nerve damage
>but wanting to heal it herself
>with cold and hot compresses
>before and after
>walking a young border collie
>who loves squirrels and snow
>and paper flying in the wind
>and with no rest in sight
>she finally tells her daughter
>about her injury
>all the while
>denying her own tears
>and promising
>never to have a stroke
>but rather
>a fatal heart attack
>at which point
>she will be dead
>and not a burden.

Gran tells the story...

March 19, 2010
Text messaging between Janet and Laura

J: Happy Birthday! WOW 23 years! Have a great one! Love you. Mom & Pop
L: Thanks!!!
J: Are you celebrating tonight?
L: Yup. I'm going out with some friends
J: Call Grandma if you can – she has been unwell lately
L: I called her today and left a message
How has she been unwell?
J: Dizziness, and throwing up and urinary tract infection according to Emerg doctor but she seems on the other side of it
L: Oh dear, okay, I hope so
J: Dorcas is also sick – under quarantine for flu-like symptoms
L: Geeez
J: We found out about both of them the same day
L: Wow how awful
J: So we need to pray for our two oldest family members
L: Yes, okay
J: I'm watching the movie 'Up' over & over again for my own mental health. Have you seen it?
L: No, I've heard its good though I'd like to see it.
J: It's great – watch for all the visual details – you'll love it
L: Will do!!
J: Buy it for your birthday and then we'll have a copy in Toronto to watch whenever – I've borrowed a copy from Lynette but definitely worth owning – all about life and love and the whole 'damn' thing – about getting old and being young and adventures
L: Okay sure Haha aww

J: I just saw a papaya in the fridge and thought of you – Our Hawaii Adventure!

L: Aw I miss papayas so much!!

J: Buy one or two or three for your birthday – a healthy way to celebrate a special day – have a papaya party – I'm going to – in your honour, of course. A mound of papaya with a candle on the top –

J: I just remembered working on Halloween Parties with you – that was fun wasn't it?

L: so fun!!!

J: Pin-the-tail-on-the … I still have the cardboard dog – great visual – you could work for Pixar

L: Hahaha aw
I just got your voicemail by the way, thanks!

J: You're welcome – yes, with your visual savvy, Pixar would be thrilled to have you!

L: Fridays we go over to Humber and use the darkroom and there is no service there

J: Okay, so I won't try to connect – are you almost there now?

L: no, home now

J: Gotcha, Have a Happy Darkroom Experience and a Happy 23rd Birthday
I love you

L: I love you!!!

Did you know …
"This is the day Mom died"

We three sisters and my daughter Laura had managed to get together to eat lunch, discuss Christmas, play crockinole and laugh together. But on a darker note, it was the day our mother had died so very many years ago. And it would be the day that my second mother, in excruciating pain on a stretcher at Sunnybrook Hospital with a broken hip, would experience the death of her life as she knew it.

After xrays, a pain block screamingly more painful than the injury itself, a catheter-insert, and an intravenous drip … plus, "was given enough morphine to kill a horse," mother Mary "drifted off into her own particular reality".

Eight hours later, the patient was wheeled off to a hallway in front of the nurses' station to wait overnight for a room. I went home at one a.m. to try and get some needed sleep.

Next afternoon, I found the crying patient still in the hallway awaiting surgery. "How would you rate your pain?" *the nurses were required to ask incessantly.* On a scale from one to ten, it was always ten – mostly emotional. I thought the patient stated that she did not want surgery, but her sons possessed a power-of-attorney document, and given the pain she was experiencing, her request did not seem rational even to sensible, practical me, and so the surgery proceeded two days after the crippling event. During the preparatory two days, relatives came to potentially say their last good-byes in the event of her demise on the operating table. But the patient survived. Only the broken femur head was discarded and a large surgical cut and very bruised ankle remained to mark the event. We never met the surgeon, even though we waited bedside for a "brief update" which was relayed to a family member to whom we are not currently speaking.

As usual, the hospital stay consisted of bad food, delayed pain meds and both good and bad company. I visited every day for two weeks, at which point the patient was transferred to Baycrest Rehab Wing "C", Floor 3, and another leg of the journey began under the care of doctor Herskoff and surrounded by sunflower prints in a private room which normally would have cost $250 extra dollars per day.

Except for a few people throwing up and causing a six-day lockdown on the floor, all went relatively well. As mentioned, and true to form, the food was terrible in spite of a personal discussion with the dietitian who appeared to be trying to do her best. We met Lingo and Mrs. Lee and a Jewish man who invited us to meetings every Friday; one who believed in God's protection as a Jew against 6 billion, and recently widowed Mrs. Fester who had "fallen down" but not broken anything.

A team consisting of occupational therapists, social worker and physiotherapist kept all of us on the move for thirty days, until Mary finally returned to her retirement residence a few days before Christmas, almost to become Mary once more. Unfortunately, when welcomed back by friends, Mary replied with a question: "where am I coming back from?"

Approximately three weeks later, on January 4th I received a call stating that Mary had fallen that morning… her right hip was broken, and we are starting the painful process once more.

"Where was I?" "Where am I?" "Where am I going?"

Welcome back.

"Glad to be back… where have I been?"

First Meeting

Sixteen years ago,
we meet at your cottage
on Weslemkoon Lake.

I am forty-nine
and you are eighty-four.
We are both Capricorns—
"salt of the earth" types.

When I comment on your unusual name,
you lead me to a biblical passage
describing a woman who sews and serves.

As you sit on the porch
drinking coffee in your bathrobe,
I mention your suddenly dead son
and my suddenly dead husband.

We also speak of green parrots
imported from Argentina.
Our interests are diverse.

You bake a pineapple pie
with graham cracker crust
I bring you truffles
from the Chocolate Messenger
in Toronto.
We are both bakers and cooks
and aspiring connoisseurs.

A sudden downpour thunderstorm
catches us by surprise
while crossing the big lake
and you are waiting at the cottage
to help us dry out and decompress.
There is no automatic washer or dryer.

And then on Christmas day
in your ninety-ninth year,
you advise that life is short,
make the most of it.
and here we are trying to do just that.

For throughout our years together,
there has been
"plenty of water under the bridge"
and I am grateful to God
for every single clichéd drop.

WATCHING

Grandma watches me on YouTube
as I make nut milk,
And she says she can tell
it's as *smooth* as silk.

Aunty watches me on YouTube
and so *very* soon,
She's making nut milk
stirring with a spoon.

Great Gran watches me on YouTube
comfy in her bed,
And *dreams* of making nut milk
but *only* in her head.

I watch myself on YouTube,
and *all* I can see,
Is a girl making nut milk
who looks *just* like me.

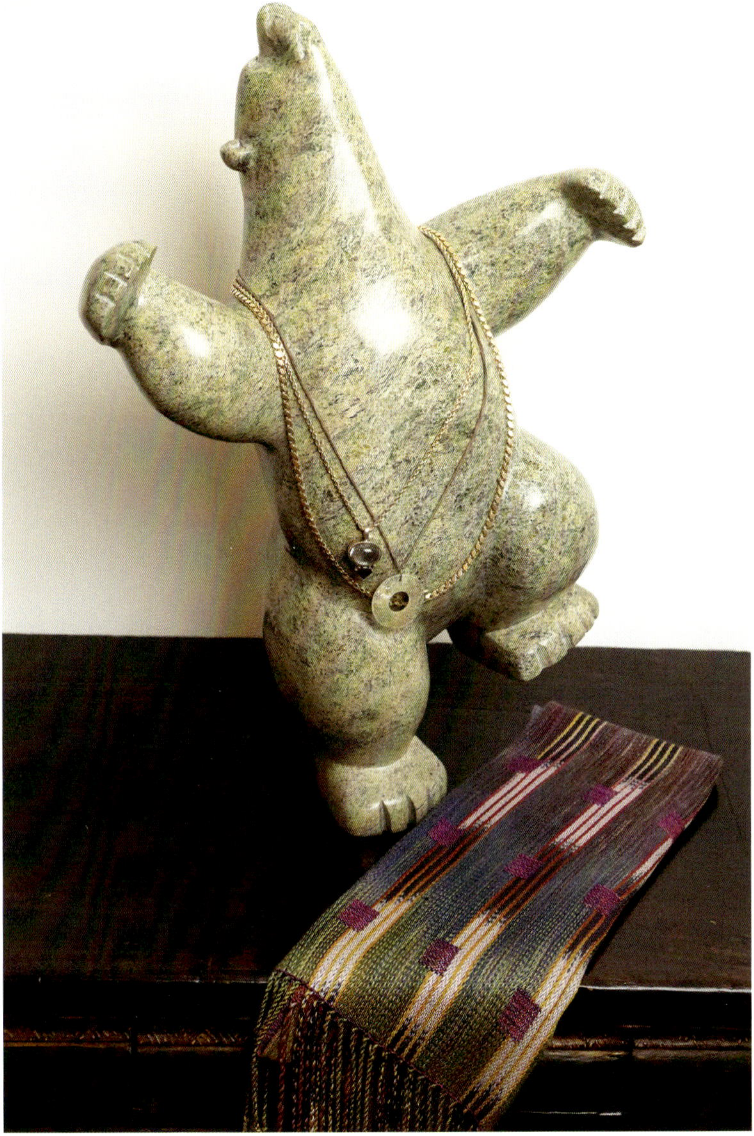

Without You

Your name is Dorcas –
An unusual name.
A biblical name.
A woman of good deeds.

Ten years ago,
we all rallied round
to share our life energy
for your 90th birthday.
Ninety candles were lit
causing a blazing inferno
that threatened to burn
down the house.
You humbly tried your best
to blow them out.

Without you ...

Richard, Loraine and Jim
wouldn't have been born
Chris and Jay wouldn't exist
nor would Debbie or David
or great grandchildren
or the next generation
And the next and the next.
None would exist without you.

I wouldn't be here sharing
This day with all of you
if Richard hadn't chosen
to marry me
And that's just for starters!

Sitting around a campfire
on a people-free beach in Hawaii
On Richard's 65th birthday
I required him to remember
65 events in his life,
as we lit 65 candles.
One by one we proceeded
And a memory
of being pulled in a sled
down the middle of an empty road
on a very dark night
lit only by the moon
and the sound of your footsteps
in the snow.
On the way to get milk
at a store lost in time.

But for you.

Vitamin Time

Tablets and caplets and gel caps
erase my daily pain
Taken at breakfast, supper and bedtime
They are placed in my hand
I can feel them, but I cannot see them.
Coffee and water assist me
in this undertaking
Crispy warm toast with grape jelly makes the medicine stay down.
I pray that my Ranitidine
continues to quell indigestion.
I am a walking/talking pharmacy.

Ranitidine 50 mg.
Metoprolol
Tartrate
Aspirin 80
Calcium 500 mg.
Reminyl
Ranitidine 150
Vitamin D 1,000
Leva/Carb 25 mg.
Hydrochlorolthiazide 25 mg.
Detrol 2 mg.
Citalopram 20 mg.

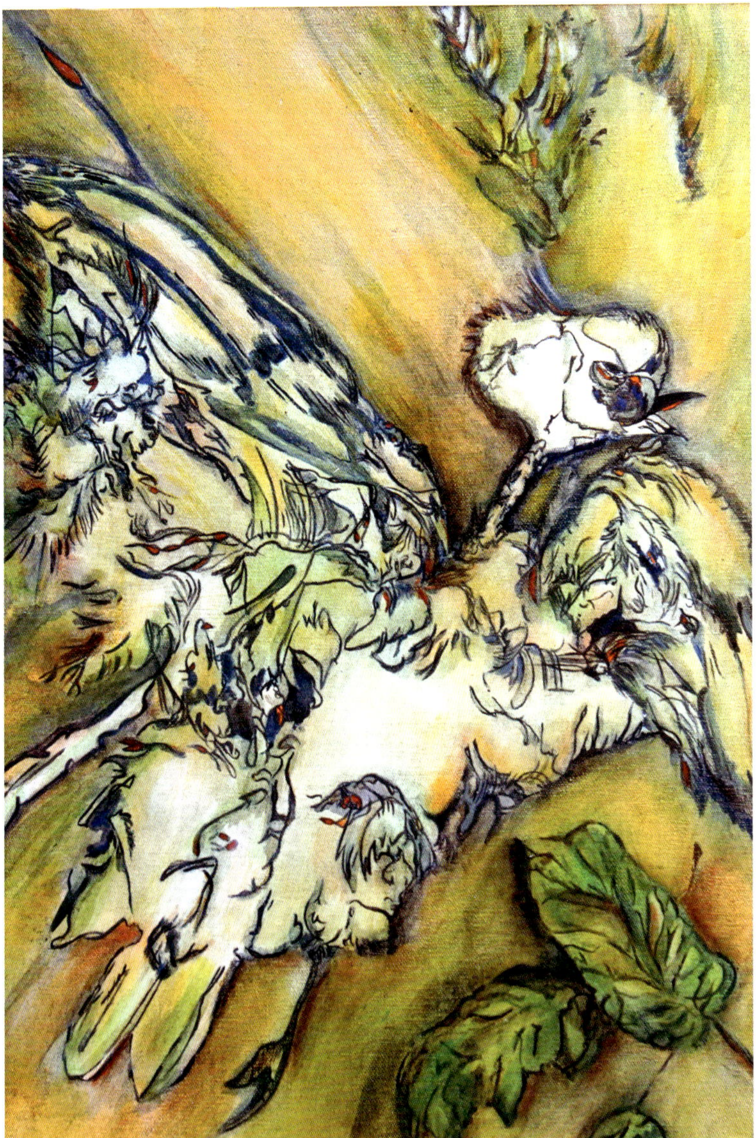

"I'm Still a Woman"

I am raised from the bed
My *New!* saturated pink-edged
For-women-only Depend
Is removed

I sit on my raised toilet seat
Waiting for assistance
I am bone-on-bone
From head to toe

Dressing is painful and shaky
My twelve-stone-disciple bracelet
Rattles

Arm holes on clothing are elusive
Neck holes and leg holes
Are not much better

I have my hair brushed up
Think about my un-lipsticked mouth
And remove my two dental plates
From their overnight Polident soak

My *New!* fresh pink-edged
For-women-only Depend
Seals itself to my body

Clothed I sit on my raised toilet seat
Waiting for my feet to be made whole
With tape and foam

Elastic and plastic
Hold toes that curve and bend
In the wrong direction

Tough elastic stockings
Compress my veins and arteries
Preventing water buildup
Around my ankles

My SAS shoes embrace my weary feet
I release the brakes from my walker
Stepping out to face my day

"I'm still a woman"

The Well-Worn Path

Your footsteps have worn
a path to our door,
and over time,
love and kindness
have compressed the clay soil
into solid brick.

You treat us to
survival soup,
custard pie,
and macaroni and cheese;
Simple fare,
and yet
profoundly comforting
to the heart and soul.

Our children have responded
to the honesty
of your caring, giving ways,
and have built you into their lives.

Simultaneously,
you have fortified each other,
accepting both strengths
and weaknesses,
turning them into positive forces.

"I love Grandma"
these simple words
uttered spontaneously
and openly,
Tell the tale.

Selfishly,
we want you to always
be here for us,
but as you get older
and physical problems arise,
we are reminded
that in one way
we are asking the impossible.

Yet in another,
we are not:
For your footsteps
have worn a permanent path
to our hearts,
and for this we thank you.

A Time

There was a time
When you could go
From Belleville to Toronto.

A Dunnville car
You drove afar
To Jackson's Point
And Nippissing.

And strode a street
In trench coat fair
With husband near
We know not where.

Argentina was a must,
Turkey, Italy, Switzerland
You stirred up dust
And buried a son.

Then came the day
When you would ask;
"Shall I see the 'Koon
Or Honolulu's shore?"

And we hastened to add;
"Yes once more,
The shores are yours
Once more."

Then joints gave out
With pain so near
And falling down
Was too far to go.

Canes and walkers
Became your friends
As to and from
Your meals you went.

Soon wheelchair bound
And sightless too
You buzzed for help
Which came to you.

And as you sit
You can vacantly stare
Or talk for ten
And dream for more
Of distant lands
With company galore
Where music
And dancing abound
And God is found.

There is a time.

From Internment to Internment

And suddenly bombs are dropping on Hawaiian soil:
Waves of hatred go out
Slam Canadian shore thousands of miles across the pacific
You lose your house, your car, your livelihood.
Sold out by the government
and sent by train to a camp in the interior.
You become a prisoner of war –
A "Jap" with a single suitcase.

Shacks – without electricity, heat,
running water or interior toilets –
protect you from the elements.
And contrast sharply with the beauty
of the surrounding countryside.

Although caged,
you sneak out
Always wondering if you will be shot as a spy
for trout fishing.

And suddenly a bomb is dropped on Japanese soil:
Waves of surrender ebb and flow
on the continents
You are free to return to your homeland of origin
or to settle in the east.
You regain Canadian citizenship
A house, a car and a job as a tailor.
The government even says it's sorry for the trouble caused
and sends you 21,000 dollars.

You hunker down in the city
Play golf
Resume fishing
And launch four tennis playing children.

And suddenly a bomb is dropped on American soil:
Massive twin towers crumble and burn
And the world is again changed forever
But you have already freed your mind
from earthly concerns.

And as the Alzheimer's progresses
Your house, and car and livelihood
are lost to you.
Fishing and golf become mental exercises
And even wandering through the neighborhood
looking for trout streams
is no longer an option.

Suddenly by drugs and on a wooden highchair,
you forget how to swallow
And are released at last on your 92nd birthday
to God's camp
To golf and fish forever.

A Lesson Worth Learning

Overcome by a profound sadness,
I weep for the past and the future
That are Now
And a feeble man
Who has become
A disheartened mind.

One who tries to rule by intimidation
But only succeeds in alienating
And creating a sense of loss.

Where is the grandfather
Who builds birdhouses?
Certainly never ours:
Nor anything to the children
Except someone to be tiptoed around
And avoided if possible.

Like ancient fossilized remains,
He has left his impression,
Instilling in others
A fresh determination
Never to become like him.

Drawn between Life and Death
I stand firmly at a distance,
Momentarily fearful
That if I get too close,
I might catch "It"
Like some dreadfully incurable disease.

But realizing a counterforce within,
So strong and only getting stronger:

Please and thank you Mr. P.H.D.,
You have taught me well.

We are All On the Move

"Are you selling the family dishes?" I boldly ask my sister.
She says "Yes, how did you know? I am leaving my house
at this exact moment."
"Sandra told me yesterday," I confess.
"You are both right about the Buddhist idea of
not attaching to things," she says.
She speaks of old towels in a garbage bag that raccoons
thought they wanted but didn't,
And an old sofa, dirty and worn without springs and
a velvet loveseat no longer loved,
and a house she doesn't want to leave.
She tells me about a male antique dealer, invited to her house
on Friday night,
after she spoke with his wife, of course.
He spent several hours evaluating her belongings and informed her
that her daughter's work is Folk Art.
"All he wanted to buy was Dad's old crock on the hearth,"
she says,
"But we did have a great conversation and he even showed me
his book."
"I forgot to offer him tea."
And I say, "Thank goodness he wasn't a Boy Scout Leader
or a Catholic Priest,"
and she laughs.
Then God enters our always-longer-than-five-minute exchange and
He has me read from my daily devotional about the temporary
nature of wealth and health and life itself.
And I send her off seeking another God Moment which is all
we really can possess,
and God's House, the only House we will never have to leave.

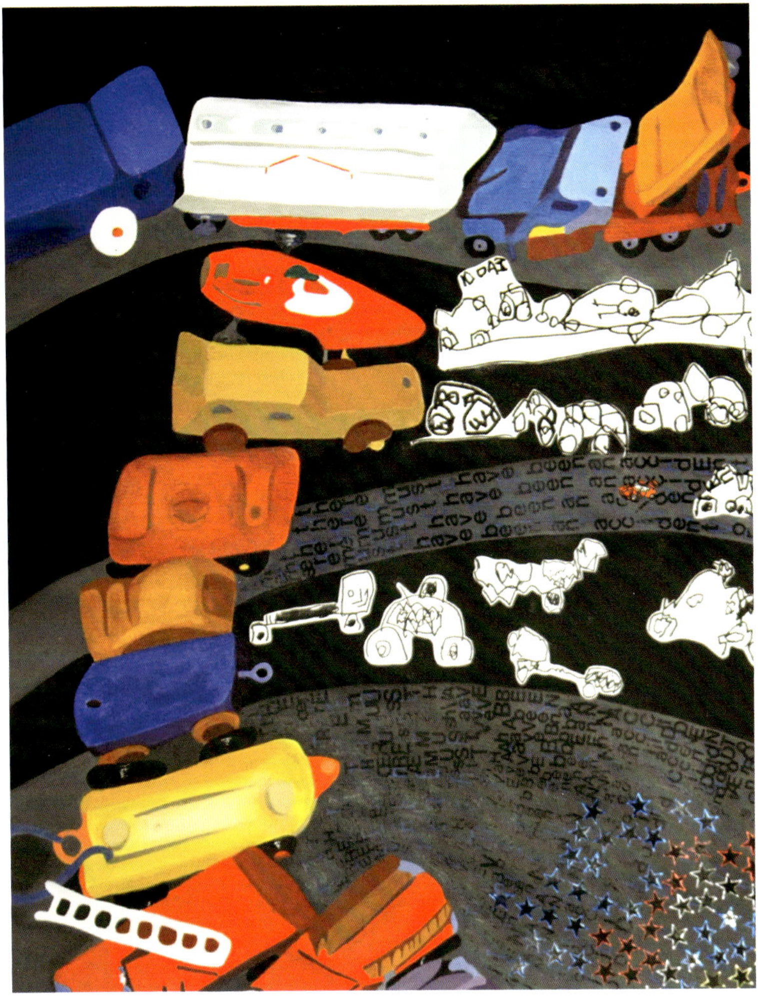
there must have been an accident

CANCER CONVERSATIONS

Janet experienced what tuned out to be a gallbladder attack while on vacation in Mexico in 2008, then again in Hawaii and at our cottage in 2009, and once more in Toronto the summer of 2010. She believed the issue was food related, but when the situation persisted and diagnosis in Toronto was inadequate we sought medical assistance in Cleveland, where the problem was identified as gallbladder – and a mammogram testing diagnosed breast cancer. The cancer was advanced, having spread to Janet's lymph nodes, and doctors pressed her to undergo massive chemotherapy, radiation and hormone treatments. But Janet did her own research. She determined there was good evidence that naturopathic alternative therapy was as effective as chemo and allopathic medicine – and that it offered a higher quality of life and an equivalent long-term survival rate. From that decision of Janet's, we experienced many *God Moments*, taking us on an amazing journey. Janet's alternative medical path resulted in cancer remission within only a few months, to her oncologist's surprise. Then cancer returned in 2015, metastasized in Janet's abdominal wall – a death sentence – but Janet experienced spontaneous healing through prayer, custom immunization and reiki therapy. It was at this point that Janet and I decided to sell our Toronto home and purchase a home in Ohio, and did so in another miracle moment. God blessed us with one more glorious season together. Cancer returned with a vengeance in January, 2017. Janet's spirit left her body to be with our Lord on the fourteenth anniversary of our marriage. March 9, 2017.

---

178 *Statistically Speaking* – Janet reviews condition and decisions.

180 *Hi Darlene* – Letter to a friend, showing courage and humor.

181 *pH 5 @ 5:25 a.m.* – Food-as-medicine path to recovery.

182 *A Good Day of Wellness* – Hope, gratitude and faith.

183 *Weighed and Measured and Labeled* – Health monitoring.

184 *Elisabeth Kübler-Ross* – Janet's Christmas turkey poem.

186 *Carrot Juice* – Food as medicine, seeks God's added direction.

187 *I Prayed to be Able to Walk* – Journal entry. Joy recalled.

188 *Only Pure Aid food* – A haiku. Food-as-medicine journey.

189 *Clean Food* – The challenging limitations of food as medicine.

190 *A Spring Haircut* – Seeking a hair cut to uplift her spirits.

193 *At the FEDEX Office* – A *God Moment:* German clinic.
195 *The Healing* – God's hand through prayer, visualization.
196 *The Party Theme is: It's a Miracle* – Our celebration.
198 *Dear Lord, I Pray* – Cancer in remission. April 30, 2011.
199 *Playing with Words* – Journal entry. God's hand.
200 *The Rosemary Connection* – Ohio moment draws memory of Molokai home blessed with rosemary bush.
201 *SOSO* – A fun ditty about Janet's food-as-medicine journey.
202 *Thank You for Your Testimony* – Cancer Group moment.
204 *Now That is an Excellent Brew* – 2nd year survival anniversary.
205 *Green Vegetables and Chamber Music* – How Janet lived life.
206 *The Cookie* – A food-as-medicine restricted life.
207 *A Personal Watermelon $5.49 Each* – Humor and flashback.
208 *Am I a Wreck?* – Journal entry self-conversation.
209 *Organic Granny Smith* – Humorous journal entry.
210 *Over My Dead Body* – Considering a "green" cemetery burial.
211 *A Veggie Burger* – Another food-as-medicine haiku.
212 *The Perfect Sin* – Last writing. Chat with a hospital janitor.
213 *Just Walking Along* – On mothers Mary and Dorcas's lives.
214 *You Can Still Make Bread* – Moments of fun, joy, courage.
217 *Janet Tomato Seed* – A fantasy wish. Of joy, humor. Legacy.
219 *A Love Greeting* – God's promise of eternal life and joy.

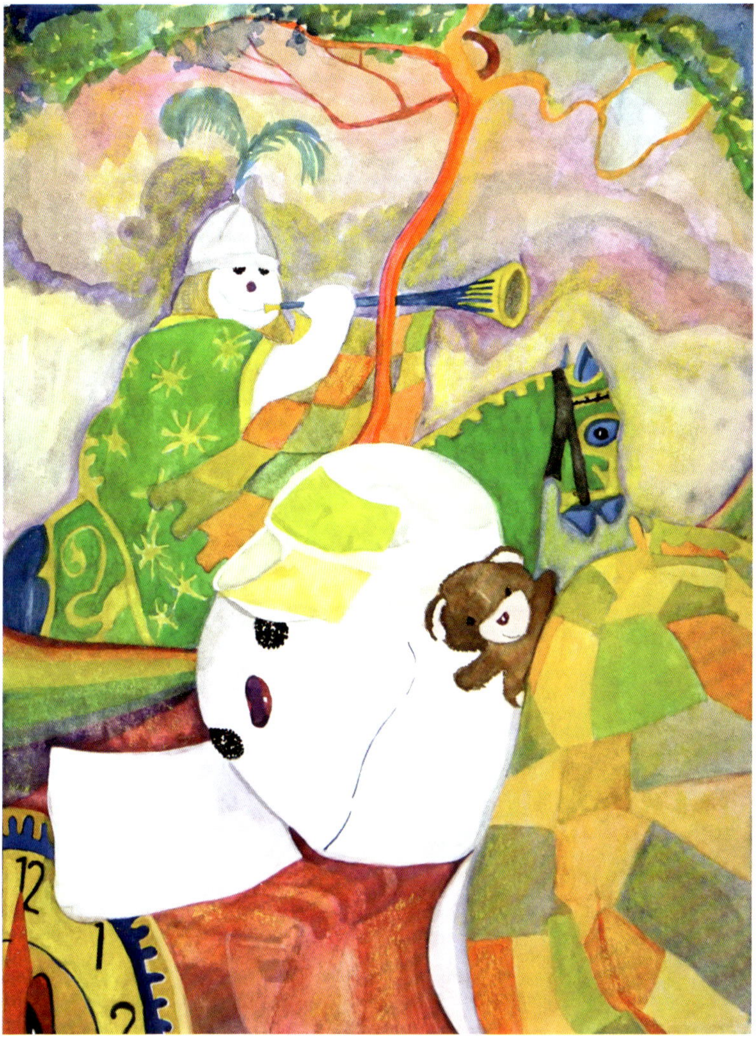
12
1
2

STATISTICALLY SPEAKING

If two hundred women
Age 61 with Stage 3 lobular
invasive breast cancer
(Estrogen positive. HER2 negative)
Are reading outdated magazines
in the allopathic practitioner's waiting room.
All are missing a
left breast, a gallbladder,
twelve lymph nodes
(eleven diseased and one healthy),
and three gallstones
found in their bile duct.
They still have a pseudo-cyst on the left lung
filled with non-cancerous debris
And a baseball sized pseudo-cyst on the pancreas,
Probably filled with non-cancerous debris
But not confirmed as yet.
They have all endured
Sixteen days of bedrest
Consumed extra-strength Tylenol every four hours
And drinking eight ounces of Gatorade
Every twenty-four hours.
Statistically speaking,
How many of these women
Will be alive in 2020?

> *Remember to: Show your work.*
> *There will be marks given for your work,*
>   *not just a correct answer.*
> *68% … 34% ….*

And then the clock starts ticking
Since the chemo train leaves the station
In twelve weeks
But only one hundred women buy into
the chemo-radiation-hormone-therapy
for-five-years ticket
The remaining hundred opt for God's love
green juice, adequate rest, exercise, sunshine
and God, our Lord's love and tender mercies.

(to be continued)

September 29, 2010

Hi Darlene –

Yes, I was a warrior when I was hospitalized: After 9 days on an I.V. drip I was having difficulty staying warm and so I wore two hospital gowns – one tied normally at the back and a second over my shoulders, tying at the front, as a cape. I called the second gown my "warrior cape" and was determined to wear it until my release. I think the nurses thought I had lost my mind.

Presently, I am also a warrior but a temporary physical ceasefire of sorts seems to have occurred as I try to re-arm my mind, body and spirit with faith, hope and love and a lot of fresh greens, exercise and good solid rest.

I call on God every day for His loving and stabilizing touch, and I am counting on Him to continue to lead me into battle.

Thank you for reaching out to me with your words of encouragement.

Janet

My "warrior cape" gave me the strength to creep into the bathroom pushing my I.V. pole.

Wolves at the door

October 1st 2010
5:25 a.m.

PH 5
Is my body cleaning out acidity overnight? (As I rest?)

I am lying in bed and God is with me.
I can touch my right ear with my left hand by going over my head without cheating by tilting my head.
I am eating broccoli, radish and alfalfa sprouts.
The thought of a burger on a bun is repugnant. (It won't be by 6 p.m.)
Red Robin Gourmet Burger be damned!
I am **not** of this world.

    Sprouts on an empty stomach --- stars before your eyes.

    There are broccoli sprout crumbs in my bed!

A Good Day of Wellness

God is with me. (He took the cramps in my leg away)
I am *not* in the hospital @ 5 a.m.
I can get out of bed by myself without pain.
There are many opportunities for acts of kindness.
I have green juice to drink courtesy of Chef Richard.
Laura is coming on Friday.
My hand can hold a pen and I am writing.
I try to learn something new every day.

WEIGHED AND MEASURED AND LABELED

The hourglass   turns

I am weighed and measured:
pH 8.0 (urine). pH 7.9 (saliva)
Pounds: 102
Fahrenheit: 97.22 (oral)
and 96.45 (saliva)
Pulse still throbbing in both wrists.
Conair 100% BORD Brush
stimulates blood and lymph flow
always in the direction of the heart.
Bathmat down
Towel up on new plastic door-hook
Water flows.
Nature's Safe jojoba shampoo (Chatsworth, California)
revitalizes.
Towel dries, 100% micro-cotton. (Made in India)
Mitchum Power-Gel protects. (Made in New York)
Hydra Me' nourishes, with 10 certified organic botanicals.
Tweezerman tweezers.
Ebony Gilligan & O'Malley seamless brief. (Made in China)
But no breast, equals no *Wacoal bra.* (Made in China)
Cotton shirt, long sleeves to cover veins. (made in Mexico)
Cotton jeans. (made in Mexico)
Nylon/Polyester vest… 100% bulletproof as usual. (Made in China)
Favorite socks. (of Unknown origin)
Black *Merrell Encore Breeze* shoes. (Michigan)

I am an international woman

the grains of sand fall to the bottom.

Elisabeth Kübler-Ross

Recently, I saw the famous death guru Elisabeth Kübler-Ross on television. She is in her seventies now and is impatient to die after experiencing a multitude of strokes. She feels as if she is, at the moment, like a plane out of the gate that is unable to take off. She just wants God whom she calls the "greatest procrastinator" to get on with things.

While reviewing literature regarding the content of her book, "On Death and Dying", I came to realize that at the tender age of twelve, I had unwittingly documented Kübler-Ross' stages of death in a poem entitled "Christmas Turkey".

The poem follows and I shall use the letters DABDA to represent the five stages of Denial and Isolation, Anger, Bargaining, Depression and Acceptance that Kubler-Ross documented in her work.

Christmas Turkey

I am a Christmas turkey	
So round, so firm, so stout,	
And I very often wonder	
Just what Christmas is all about.	(A) Acceptance
Why do people eat us turkeys?	
So kind, so dear are we,	(D) Denial and Isolation
Why can't they eat a duck or two	
Instead of eating me?	(B) Bargaining

Worry, worry, worry,
That's all I ever do,
When the Christmas season
Comes around
And even New Year's too.   (D) Depression

Will I be killed and roasted
Like many a friend of mine,
So greedy little children
Can merrily sit and dine?   (A) Anger

But I am a Christmas turkey
And there's nothing I can do,   (A) Acceptance
But hope that Christmas never comes (B) Bargaining
And I'm not a feast for you!   (D) Denial

   Criticism of Kubler-Ross' work has focussed on the danger of expecting a predictable path for those experiencing a life event such as the death of a loved one or a similar emotion-fraught transition phase. As is the case with my turkey, stages can occur in a multitude of orders and can even present themselves simultaneously.

   Several years ago, when this poem was published in a grade school booklet of poems, I was required to remove the words "kill" and "greedy", essentially eliminating all of my turkey's anger and sense of injustice. Such editing only served to make me angry and did not serve the purpose of documenting the true feelings associated with death and dying.

   My thanks go to Elisabeth Kubler-Ross for providing a forum for discussion regarding all of the emotions encountered in a lifetime on this planet and I pray for her speedy and painless deliverance to God.

CARROT JUICE

Wounds are still fresh
As we say Hallelujah to carrot juice
And we buy the Green Star Juicer
And the mason jar vacuum sealer
Ready for fall, no-steam-ahead production.

Then we learn something new
About acidity and alkalinity
And the word called a *pH Miracle*
And suddenly cucumber and celery juice rules
But is slow to materialize.

Fear and doubt and impatience creep in
In spite of knowing in our hearts
That we must wait upon the Lord --
Wait upon the Lord for His direction
And His Healing Hand.

Remembering Socrates forced to drink the deadly hemlock
As the dreaded words Adriamycin, Paxil and Taxol
And five years of Herceptin
Drifting ever so gently into the dark, rain-filled night.

Fear of chemotherapy – why so profound?
Chemotherapy == death
Why not sit people down to a glorious, hand-made
glowing fresh salad of greens instead of
sticking an I.V. into their arms and killing their immune system.
Does God want this for me?
Ultimate act of humility… of surrender?

I Prayed to be Able to Walk

I prayed
To be able
To walk
Where I had never
Walked before:
And
I did.

I prayed to walk where
I had never walked before
God-willing, I did

And that led to this….

Took me straight back
To my x-country skiing days.
Cream-colored birch
Leaves on the trees
In the middle of the woods

And being at Weslemkoon
In winter: walking on water –
Frozen, of course!

Where were we?

Only Pure Aid food

Only Pure Aid food
Supplied by God like Manna
From heaven above

Clean Food

After days and days of green juice
And green soup
I am desperate for chew-food:

I head to the local Chinese restaurant
For a melange of vegetables
With brown rice but no baby corn or mushrooms
And no fried spring roll appetizer.
I wait ten minutes
What I get is white rice
And a piece of chicken skin
Which I definitely did not order
As well as a multitude of microforms
In my blood which I see under the microscope
And find appalling
As I accumulate a pile of paper scraps
From the fortune cookies
That make mindless sense
Along with lucky numbers and random words
I am compelled to return to *The Source*
Knowing that *"when the perfect comes,
the partial will pass away."*

1 Corinthians 13:19

A Spring Haircut

After thirty years of cutting my own hair,
I decide to visit a hair salon.

My number one rule is:
When the deed is done, my hair will be tied back.

All I want is an uplift,
A lightening of the hair load
Nothing fancy or extreme.

My new hairdresser tricks me into trust:
she decides not to cut to shoulder length,
but to trim.

Sounds good.

And so the wash and trim begin.

She talks about the rule for bangs
which I have broken,
And suggests a grow-in period
of six to eight months.

Sounds a little too optimistic to me
but I do not convincingly object.

We share dead husband stories:
More trust is established.
I even close my eyes
as she asks permission to execute some "feathering."
The blow dry and style are uneventful.

I head for the front of the salon
and try to tie my hair back:
Large pieces of "feathered" hair do not comply.
I ask my hairdresser's recommendations:
Bobby pins, hairspray and tucking behind my ears
are her best suggestions.

I see her now as Edward Scissorhands
in a topiary frenzy
giving me a Spring haircut in the dead of Winter.

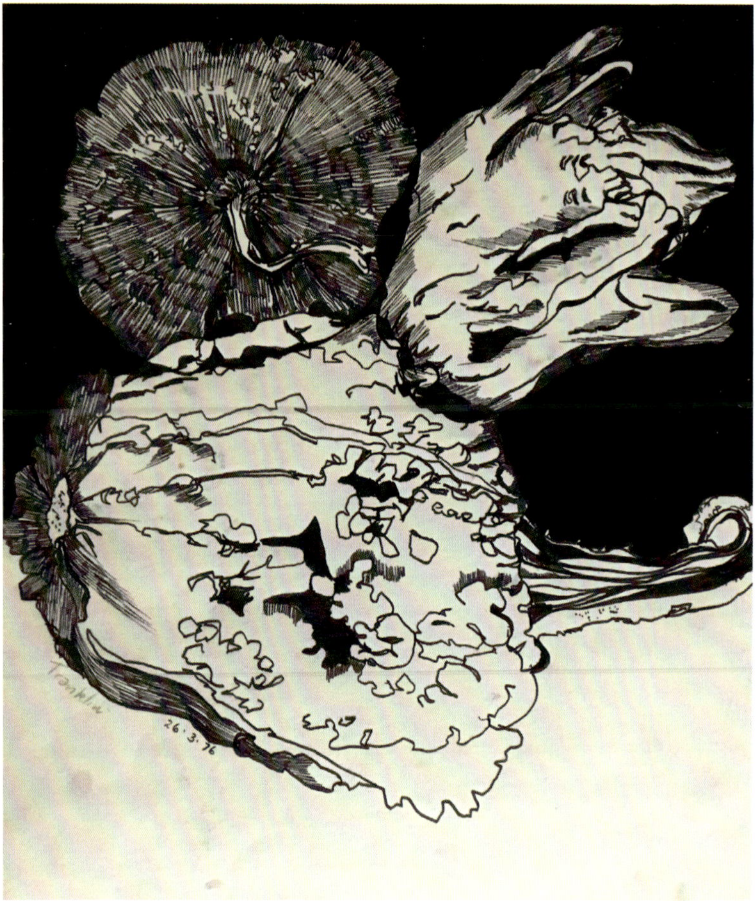
Franklin
26.3.76

AT THE FEDEX OFFICE

We arrive at the airport FEDEX office.
I need to provide a urine sample to send to Germany.

The washroom is monitored by airport security:
It is not a public facility.

A snowstorm rages on outside:
Snow Road is more treacherous than ever.

Kathy, the FEDEX attendant, senses our desperation:
She decides to break the rules.

I and my urine sample cup are escorted to the washroom.
I have exactly enough urine to fill the cup –
No more, no less.

I thank the security guard and reveal my cancer status
while telling him that potentially he has saved my life.

I then inform the FEDEX attendant
about the details of our dilemma.
She thought that too much coffee was involved.

By this time, I am crying.

After helping us fill out the paperwork,
She says she will pray for me
and assures me that I am going to be fine.

Without a doubt, God's total love visible in the world.

(continued)

FBM-PHARMA Gmbtl Geseliscaft fur biologishe Medizin

Dear Mr. Foster,
we've received the blood this morning, everything's okay!
I will inform you as soon as I know the completion date of
the medications.
Best regards
Sabine

Out of the depths have I cried unto thee. Oh Lord

THE HEALING

-go deep with God

-allow Him to nurture ME
 as I have nurtured others

-allow God to lead
-envision warm oil being
 poured on me

-I see myself under
 God's protective wing

-God is vacuuming up the random
 cancer cells and removing
 them as light

-God turning *darkness* into light
 and then a healing can result

The party theme is: It's a Miracle

Thank you for being born, so I can take this opportunity to invite you to our first semi-annual Birthday Party.

The party theme is: **It's a Miracle.**
And we shall gather together to celebrate our lives through music, art, movement, and storytelling.   *Sharing.*

We will play variants of classic party games like musical chairs, pin-the-tail-on-the-donkey, have a treasure hunt, food on a spoon, and fill-in-the-blank stories… *SILLY SAGAS.*

Come hungry, but not starving, for the purpose of the evening will be to graze on samples of the freshest, healthiest food that the world has to offer.

Be prepared to drink only iodized water (the finest on the planet) and fresh juices from fruit and veggies which hopefully you will bring, and which will be processed on the spot with the aid of our in-house juice expert, Richard Foster.

Grains will be cooked, but everything else will be raw and cold, veering away from meat, standard sugars, dairy, eggs and standard condiments. *What is left?!?* I hear you cry. Well actually a multitude of healthy, satisfying foods that enhance the functioning of your brain and heart, because at this celebration, we need your brain and heart to be functioning at maximum capacity.

The fact that we are all still able to set aside our differences and gather together, will be part of the miracle. Sharing with each other and our children, in all their glory, will be the focus of the event.

The party will have a distinct beginning @4 p.m. and end @7 p.m. And so, please be on time. All games will be approximately half an hour … and so… we will have time for 4 - 6 games, plus food breaks. I will set up a program of events.

The fact that we are alive and well enough to plan this party is truly a miracle and we want to share our love, hope and sense of joy with you.

Gifts must consist of something raw, unprocessed, preferably organic. I will provide: a fruit tray, a green salad with lemon and olive oil dressing, and a grain dish.

Come for the moment, but stay a few hours!

DEAR LORD, I PRAY:

I know You have numbered my days
And as I walk through the valley of the shadow,
I ask that my journey be a longer one
(perhaps 24 more years?)
Yet always in Your company.
I see Your beauty in the flowering trees
And want to continue to hold Your hand
Feeling peace and joy
In the midst of a suffering world.
No pets, plants or laundry shall take my eyes from You.

Thank You for all of Your Blessings.

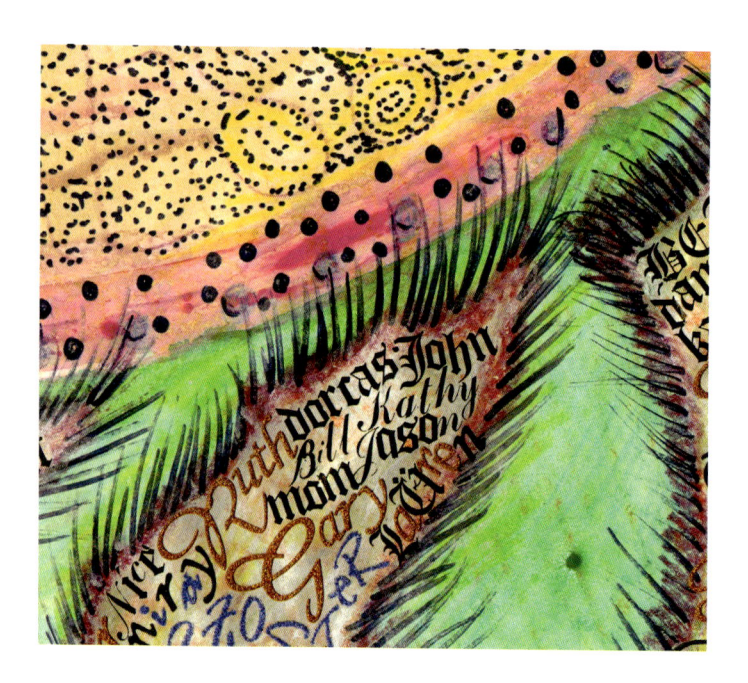

PLAYING WITH WORDS

Yesterday when I awoke at six a.m. or so, I was compelled to examine my current relationship with food. I wanted to write a haiku based on the fact that I'm not supposed to chew my food, but instead, I'm to puree it and essentially drink it. All of my salads need to be put in the Vitamix. I'm very resistant to this course of action, but I have lost as much weight as I can afford, and am actually afraid to get on a scale without three or four layers of winter clothing on my body. I think I weigh about one hundred and fifteen pounds.

Anyway, getting to the point, I noticed that the word "food" was unusual because it had few words that rhyme with it, and co-exists with many words in the English language that look the same but are not pronounced the same way. "Good"', "hood" and "stood" for example, are not rhyming friends of "food", and so I went looking for "friends" of the word 'food' that were spelled the same way with "ood". I was hard pressed to find any such words and returned to "God is good" in my mind when I needed comforting. After considerable thought and allowing my mind to go all over the English language map, I had managed to come up with "brood", "mood" and the potentially imaginary word "rood". "Rood" sounded like a word and looked like a word, but I had no idea about its meaning. After looking in the Merriam-Webster site online, I learned that "rood" means:

> A cross or crucifix symbolizing the cross on which Jesus Christ died; specifically: a large crucifix on a beam or screen at the entrance to the chapel of a church.

My word play, based on the premise that God is Good and that food is a weird word, led me where it should have – straight to the cross of Jesus Christ. (in essence, all of my beginnings and endings are covered) For He alone is my Alpha and my Omega.

Amen

The Rosemary Connection

And we go to Treehugger's Café:
Laura passes me a sprig of rosemary
I take it home to dry it out
To add to my jar of vacuum-sealed rosemary
Rosemary leaves drop to the floor
I pick two up and pop them in my mouth
And I am chewing on them as I walk
down our street to our mailbox with our key
I find a U.S. Post Office box labeled "Schaefer"
And know that it has travelled five thousand miles
I return to our kitchen and open the box
A large sprig of rosemary appears.

Along the margin of this piece, Janet wrote the following:

**Is
Rosemary
a cancer
food?**

**I feel a
sense of
loss and
sadness.
I miss
my valiant
Molokai
rosemary
bush.**

SOSO

God is very good
Choo-choo food forbidden
Til the noo-noo year.

    so-o-o-o
God is so-so good
Choo-choo food no-no-no
Till the noo-noo year.

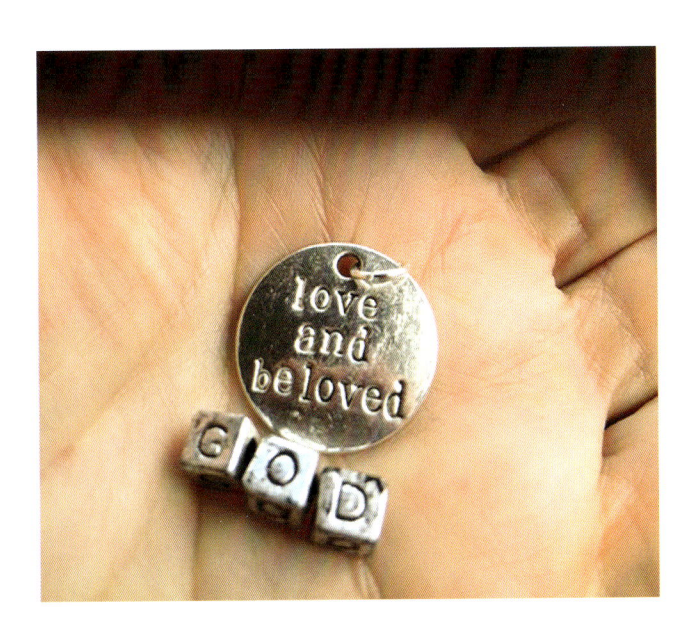

so-0000   so-0-0
    so-0-0-0

Thank You for Your Testimony

Once more I sign up for a permanent name tag
and decide to fully participate in Cancer Group
on a day when most choose silent contemplation.

After a reading of my recent favourite
2 Corinthians 4: 7-18
the question arises:
What is meant by "bring us into his presence"?
and I tell about my morning ritual upon my knees;
a gratitude moment of getting down and up
which I actually did not do on that particular day
and how surprised I am by my usual behaviour
so revealing in its simplicity
including verbalized prayer
that varies dramatically
depending on my emotional state.

But someone points out that silent prayer
is perhaps better because Satan cannot intervene
and I ponder the veracity of this revelation.

I see myself as dust ready for the Dyson
with only a somewhat tarnished silver heart
remaining after the housecleaning.

I hope that when God comes to retrieve
what is left of me
He will with open arms and eyes
look directly into my heart
and find it so full of Christ's goodness
that He says: "Thank you for your testimony"
and I shall say "Thank You" in return.

2 Corinthians 4: 7-18
(Important in full but still needs some clarification.)
However, I totally get this part, (16-18)
So we do not lose heart. Though our outer self is wasting away, our inner self is being renewed day by day. For this light momentary affliction is preparing for us an eternal weight of glory beyond all comparison, as we look not to the things that are seen but to the things that are unseen. For the things that are seen are transient, but the things that are unseen are eternal.

Now that is an excellent brew

if I do say so myself.
Very smooth – yes – very smooth.

At 7 a.m. I phone my husband who is in the shower in Florida. We confirm that we are both still on the planet having survived the night.

I rise and drink 24 ounces of ionized water with "phour" salts added. My bowel movement consists of green-as-Canada-goose poop, and then I get my hot and cold shower which takes me to Denmark and back.

I then realize that my 2nd year cancer anniversary isn't just all about me. I make four gratitude phone calls to the alternative medical support members of my "team". I leave messages for three and connect with one.

We talk about down-sizing, teeter totters, mercury in retrograde, connections to our fathers, smoking addiction, a new beginning in Beachwood, and the fits and starts of a cancer journey.

We acknowledged our life energy and staying on track, and the importance of the tiniest grain of quinoa: first on a white plate, then on a fork, and then in the mouth for protein and energy to run my body – a body which belongs to a God who provides all, and appreciates my acceptance of his gifts. Gifts including people, food, housing, rain as well as furnace repairmen and plumbers who will come next week.

I pray humbly on my knees, savoring a quart of green juice and then I am off to lunch with family to a new restaurant. I welcome a new adventure on this God-given day that has never been before.

Green Vegetables and Chamber Music

I went to the Saturday Hudson Farmers Market on the green to buy romaine lettuce, zucchini and broccoli. I took four dollars in quarters from the car with me since I only had one twenty-dollar bill in my "American" wallet.

After surveying the entire market, I determined that four dollars was inadequate even though I did taste a tiny sample of chocolate covered orange peel for free and listened to chamber music in sun-dappled glory also for nothing.

I was tempted to pay some kids across the street for some pink lemonade which I did not intend to drink, but decided not to encourage them with my fifty cents or to give them a lecture on how nasty sugar is for you. No sense in spoiling everybody's fun.

Back in the car I took out my last twenty and headed back to the market area where zucchini and broccoli reduced my twenty to fifteen. I then sat down to listen to the quartet playing chamber music and with a generous heart, placed my fifteen dollars in their jar. When I left the house, I had no idea that I would be buying green vegetables and chamber music, but come to think of it, the combination is absolutely perfect.

THE COOKIE

At the funeral reception
tea and sandwiches
and lavish trays of cookies appear
but I don't drink tea or eat bread
and I most certainly am not to eat cookies:
after all, sugar feeds cancer.

But I am allowed to sample one cookie
which becomes one kind of cookie
which means I can eat six or seven
since they are small
with poppy seeds and lemon rind
and very homemade.

And when I venture to my sister's table
where she has been drinking tea
and eating sandwiches,
I see that she also is eating only one cookie:
the one with poppy seeds and lemon rind.

A Personal Watermelon $5.49 Each

I fell in love with you immediately:
so small and cute – perfect for
one person living with another
who is repulsed by watermelon.
Thin rind, deep juicy pink interior
edible seeds and definitely tasting
BIOLOGIQUE/ORGANIC

I see a chubby–cheeked child
still in baby shoes
next to her brother on the swing
indulging to her heart's content
and I thank God for
Jeffrey METTLER Farms and His gift
of MINI WATERMELON.

AM I A WRECK?

  No,
but I was one.

I am now
being slowly
but surely
repaired
by the loving hands
of God.

Death has no hold on me
in spite of my obsession with Joe Black!

End of Conversation

ORGANIC GRANNY SMITH
Artisan Stemilt Since 1989

Every morning lately, I have been making smoothies consisting of half of a large cucumber, half of an unpeeled lemon, three large sticks of celery with chlorophyll rich leaves, and half of a very large organic granny smith apple. Next, I have been adding cilantro, parsley, romaine lettuce, kale, collard greens, and green pepper, beet and carrot tops… depending on availability. Lastly, a half or whole avocado is added to keep the mixture from separating, and to include necessary fat. The avocado and apple always have very small plastic labels indicating that they are organic. And which I always remove them immediately before juicing.

This morning, I got my shower and washed my hair before making our smoothy breakfast. As usual, I emerged from the shower stall and while standing in front of the sink, proceeded to apply underarm deodorant. Without my glasses, I noticed something white sticking in my armpit. Upon removal, and placement of my eyeglasses, the small piece of plastic turned out to be an organic granny apple label. Somehow, this "find" was disconcerting, but also amusing. Truly we do seem to become what we eat.

> ***Question:*** *How? Rest assured, I make smoothies fully clothed. My armpit has not seen the light of day since 2010 when it was exposed by a hospital gown.*

OVER MY DEAD BODY

My life has come to this:
The highlight of my day
Is when I bury my daily collected
compost as deeply as possible in the ground.
No meat, dairy or eggs
Just pure fruit and vegetable scraps.

And when I am finished with this body,
A mere speck of a scrap in the larger scheme of things.
I wish to be placed in a rattan or willow
biodegradable basket from England
And buried next to a river
which means not in the Mt. Pleasant Cemetery
But not too close to the river
Should it flood,
but then again…
And when snugly under six feet of black earth "virgin" soil,
you may place three logs from the "Koon" on top
After you have seeded them with oyster mushrooms
for the Fall and morels for the Spring.
Should you ever visit me,
Cut a mushroom, or wait in season leaving my "cell" intact for
next year.
Knowing that I love you, and my current location and situation.

Where is this river location?
Still looking – T.B.A.

A Veggie Burger

I feel a haiku coming on…
    Most veggie burgers
        have a low self-esteem because
            they're trying to be something they are not!

A veggie burger
God's greens, three soups, a half salad,
With high self-esteem.

The Perfect Sin

And after my ascites tap a man named John
comes to take away my five litres of excess fluid
and he says he wishes that he could heal everyone
in this area of the hospital just like Paul could

   and he looks to the left and to the right
   as if he shouldn't have mentioned Paul

and then David and Bathsheba enter the conversation
and Daniel who prayed consistently three times a day

   and he looks to the right and to the left
   as if he shouldn't be talking about Daniel

and then he confesses his desire for perfection
to please God and we try to talk him out of his precept
and then the real truth about his personal sin emerges
and it involves pork – you know – specifically baby back ribs

   and he looks to the left and the right
   as if he shouldn't have said baby back ribs

and we shake hands and I tell him I will meet him in heaven
but not too soon since it's all about the journey not the destination
and only God knows who will be chosen after many are called
having been forgiven for eating baby back ribs

   and upon leaving we are not looking right or left but at each other
   as we contemplate finding and eating John's very favourite food

Amen and I totally love you God

Just Walking Along

On my way out,
Do not feed me Reese's Peanut Butter Cup
or Cheezies or pureed Wonder Bread.

Do not call me "cute" or your "favourite"
Because I will not be.

Do not rest my weary bones
on a fancy electric air mattress
so my backside is
a little less sore than it already will be.

The pain will keep me up and moving.

Do not make me look '"beautiful"
with a scarf and a brooch
from the Dollar Store
and a new hairdo that
I cannot see.

Just aim me towards The Door
with my heart racing
after a long workout on a treadmill
and I promise to walk along forever
holding God's hand.

WHEN YOU HAVE CANCER, YOU CAN STILL MAKE BREAD

When you have cancer, you can still make bread

Attend a duck processing workshop

Go to a clambake

Learn how to cold compost

Move from a townhouse in Ohio and a house in Toronto to a 1970s house of glass and light and Black-eyed Susans

Have two teeth and all amalgams extracted and one implant

Grow your hair down to your waist like Lady Godiva or a mermaid

Swim in your clothes

Plan a dinner party on Bayview Avenue for 13 family members in 5 minutes

Go roller skating and break your arm

Go bowling and think your middle finger is broken

Go to the zoo and have a surprise slide event

Watch a play called "The Adams Family" at least 5 times

Go to the theater and end up in the hospital emergency department with a husband who got food poisoning and fell down the theater stairs

Have God show up directly after learning about this exchange of information

Meet two bad occupational therapists and one good one

Find a place to bury yourself and then change your mind

Have God show up while getting an ascites tap

Regain the strength in your right leg so you can drive again

Have a glitter LOVE tattoo put on your right arm and be given a repurposed leather bookmark with the word "Love" on it... because "God knows exactly what you need"

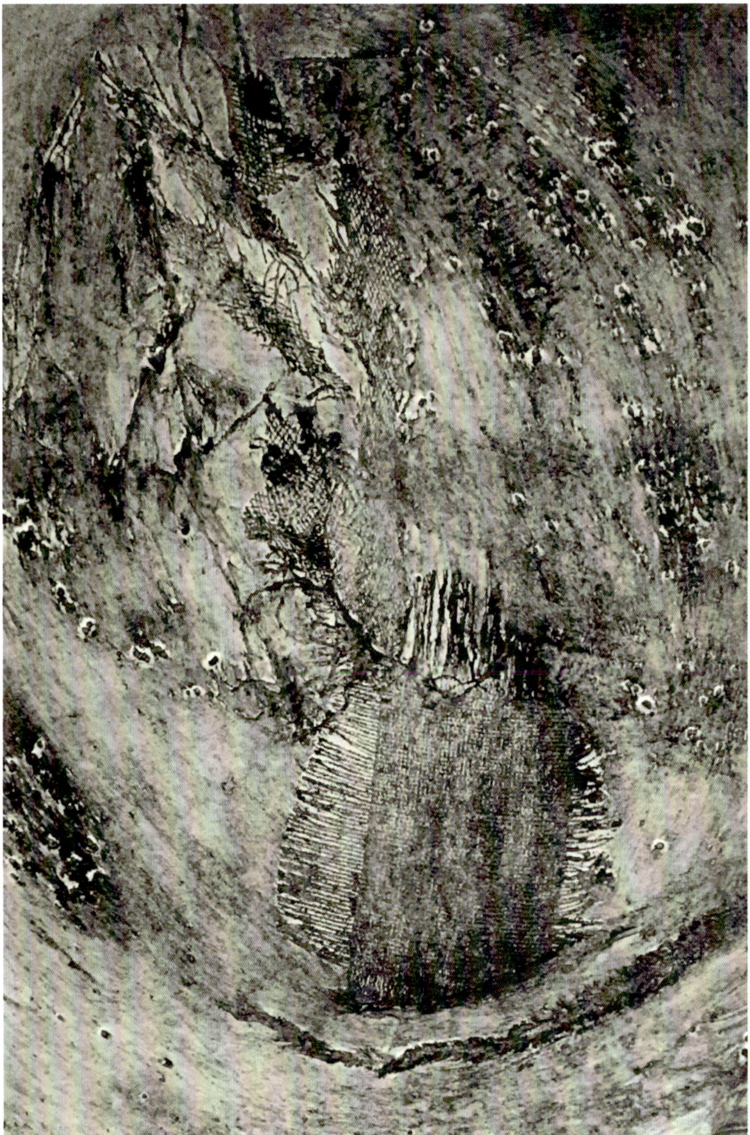

JANET TOMATO SEED

If I had my way,
I would cross the country on foot
and plant cherry tomatoes all along the way.
Crossing the country with native plants.

Massive garden salads.

Cherry tomatoes and Texas sage
Cherry tomatoes and pink hibiscus
Cherry tomatoes and Ohia Lehua
Cherry tomatoes and Ti leaves

Seeds in the ocean over the railing,
Cherry tomatoes with sea weed and salmon.

Wild, Organic Cherry Tomatoes, sundried and
lightly coated with oregano, raw extra virgin olive oil
worth mega dollars an ounce.

And my cherry tomatoes would grow
so gloriously tall, all the spirits and angels in heaven
would be feasting on cherry tomatoes.

And my picture would be put in the paper
and on the internet, known not as the Tomato Queen
but as Janet Tomato Seed.

My cherry tomatoes would grow everywhere.

Become the cure for breast cancer.

Come join me. Sit and eat a cherry tomato salad.

→ *you are cured.*

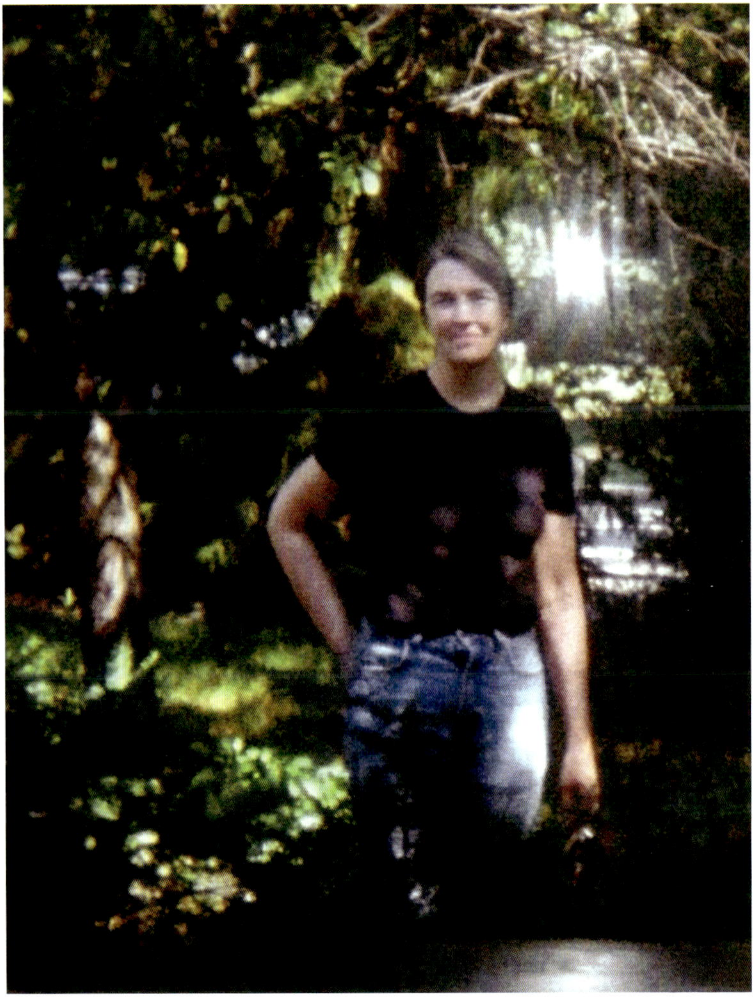

A Love Greeting

Hello to love who's knocking at our door;
Sproutings, buddings; all bursting forth anew.
The sun shines, the rain falls on...

Acknowledgments

In early May, I called Paul Kelly, founder and publisher of St. Lynn's Press, to ask if he would consider taking on this book project. And in what I call a *God Moment*, Paul shared his compassionate heart with me, and his commitment to bring Janet's book to life with me. And so, with gratitude to Paul for his guidance and blessed heart, along with the gifts of editor Catherine Dees and talents of graphic designer Holly Rosborough, we've been able to publish this book for Janet.

It's with gratitude that flows from my heart that I acknowledge the love, support and encouragement of my family as I fulfill my mission to celebrate Janet's creative life: Janet's children, Adam and Laura Franklin; my sons, Jay and Chris Foster; Janet's sisters, Marion and Sandra, and brother, Gary; and my sister, Loraine Miller.

I'm especially indebted to my daughter, Laura, for her tireless efforts in managing so much of what I could never have faced alone, and for her diligence in gathering together boxes of her mother's writings without which this book would not have been possible in such a short timeframe. I will always cherish the afternoon we spent together while I read to Laura all of my early selections of her mothers work that I was considering for this book. And for her feedback. There was a profound sharing of emotions that day, and throughout the several week-long periods these past few months when Laura came to Ohio to support my needs, including planting her mother's vegetable garden together this spring. Janet's spirit presence has been with us throughout this time. Surrounding us with her love. Drawing us closer in our grieving, and sharing, hearts.

It isn't possible to thank everyone who touched Janet's life and shaped the material Janet created in this book. Nor is this page adequate space to thank so many who have supported me in this work of love…but it's my hope and intention that the few noted here can symbolize the many.

No words are adequate to honor our dear friends Scotty and Lynette Schaefer for their friendship, love and ministry to us over the past eighteen years, and for their act of heart to immediately get on a plane from Hawaii to be with us in our greatest moment of need. To Frank Sizer, for his love and spiritual presence for Janet and for me over many years. And I will always be indebted to Janet's Team: Cindy Destasio, Rhondalynn Smith-Brustosky, Cindy Wheatcraft and Tom Frazer, who gave us hope and joy throughout Janet's seven-year cancer journey. To my dear friends Charlotte Turcotte, Barbara Munley Miranda and Bernie Krzys, who have always given their all for me. And to cousins John and Kathy Dunnett, who walked the cancer path with us, so openly sharing their love, insights and encouragement.

And to my Christian brother and dear friend Denny Zaverl, who has been my rock of spiritual and emotional support throughout this journey, and for more than two decades of my life.

Richard

About the Author

Janet Isobel Davies was born in Toronto, Ontario, Canada, on January 10, 1949 and died in Moreland Hills, Ohio, on March 9, 2017. Janet was a teacher, artist, poet and mother. She graduated from Toronto Teachers' College in 1969, and taught second grade students in the Toronto public school system for eight years, during which time she married her high school sweetheart, Tom Franklin. They had two children together, Adam and Laura. With a desire to combine her love of education with her love for art, Janet went back to school for a second degree, graduating from the University of Toronto with a BA in Fine Art. Janet didn't return to classroom teaching once her children arrived, but remained a consummate teacher, pouring her nurturing and artistic energies into her family and the children in her community. Tom Franklin died unexpectedly in 1995.

As someone who cared deeply about building every child's self-esteem, Janet helped launch a pioneering After-Four educational program in her Leaside/Bennington Heights neighborhood school, a program she managed for more than a decade. Throughout her life, she expressed her artistic talents in multiple media, from hand-sewn puppets, to collage, to oil on canvas, to 3-D sculptures. She was a gifted writer, in poetry, short stories and journals, revealing her curiosity about everyday life, nature, and the human condition. A passionate gardener, Janet planted, rescued, tended, photographed – and rejoiced in – the natural world around her.

Janet was a lifelong learner and spiritual seeker, developing a deep and abiding Christian faith, which became the core of her being during the last two decades of her life. She found a partner in faith and in life with Richard Foster. In 2003, Janet and Richard were married on Molokai, Hawaii. Janet was diagnosed with advanced breast cancer in 2010. She chose to pursue a holistic, naturopathic course of care. With periods of near-miraculous remission, she and Richard were gifted with seven more years of active life together until her death 2017.